SIMPLY SEASONAL

Claire Macdonald's
SIMPLY SEASONAL
Delicious Recipes for Year-round Informal Entertaining

Shsanah

Happy Days at Aigas

& Happy Birthday

love Lucy
x

2014

BIRLINN

This edition published in 2012 by
Birlinn Limited
West Newington House
10 Newington Road
Edinburgh EH9 1QS

www.birlinn.co.uk

First published in 2002 by Bantam Press
a division of Transworld Publishers

ISBN 978 1 78027 083 8

British Library Cataloguing-in-Publication Data
A catalogue record for this book is available from the British Library

Printed and bound in China

For Godfrey
Alexandra and Philipp
Isabella and Tom
Meriel and
Hugo

Acknowledgements

Most heartfelt thanks for the roles they play in my life are due to Godfrey, to Isabella, and to Minty Dallmeyer.

New in my working life, but extremely important and vital for the republication of this book, great thanks to all working at the publisher, Birlinn, and to Jeremy Westwood, my agent and good friend.

Contents

Introduction

This book is an acknowledgement of the increasing trend for less formal entertaining. Of course there are, and will always be, the exceptions where a degree of formality fits the occasion, but for the most part – and thankfully – the three-course dinner-party is a thing of the past. However, we can rethink our attitude towards entertaining to make life simpler. Most of us love to entertain our families and friends, but we seem to have less and less time to do so.

In this book I have suggested dishes and menus for the four seasons of the year that can be cooked and/or prepared in advance. Often, the main courses consist of one-dish recipes and need only a mixed-leaf salad to accompany them, or a vegetable which can be steamed, dressed, and eaten at room temperature. Steamed broccoli, for instance, can be cooked then simply dressed with olive oil and lemon juice in the morning ready for supper that day. You will find in this book recipes for meat, game, fish, and plenty for vegetarians.

The seasonal theme isn't new to me: my first book was called *Seasonal Cooking*, and up here where I live, in Skye, we are surrounded by growers of seasonal vegetables and fruit – and most are grown organically. This is what I think of as eating for health. I loathe and deplore the supermarket culture, with the exception of our local Co-op in Broadford – and, I must say, I do love a trawl around Waitrose when down south. But supermarkets and politicians are death to the subject of food and eating. Luckily, more of us are becoming aware of these facts, and it is ever easier to buy fresh, locally grown fruit and vegetables, even in cities through the wonderful Farmers' Markets. Politicians of every persuasion will ignore the most glaringly obvious facts, and turn conveniently blinded eyes when it suits them. The only example I will give here is the continued import of meat, particularly pig meat, from countries where the laws of raising the animals are vastly inferior to the laws that govern our own farmers and producers.

I hope very much that you enjoy reading this book, and cooking from it, because I have loved writing it!

Jerusalem artichoke soup with scallops 8

Roast red pepper, tomato and chilli soup 9

Broccoli and lemon soup 10

Blue cheese rarebit on fresh pears with fried walnuts 11

Quails' eggs, avocado and crispy bacon salad with herb dressing 12

Potted crab with Melba toast 13

Lime-marinated fresh and smoked salmon in *crème fraîche*, dill and
    cucumber, with pink peppercorns 15

Herb crêpes with smoked herring roe, cucumber and *crème fraîche* 16

Game terrine with herb jelly 17

Sautéed chicken livers with garlic, apples and balsamic vinegar 19

Spicy hummus with carrot sticks 20

Marinated grilled aubergine slices with tomato and chilli sauce 21

Spaghetti with white crabmeat, olive oil, garlic, chilli and parsley 23

Salmon fillets with watercress and shallot sauce 24

Hot-smoked salmon fishcakes with lime and shallot sauce 25

Baked marinated tuna steaks with Parmesan pasta 27

Spicy red fish stew 28

Smoked haddock creamy stew with shallots, saffron and baby spinach 29

Chicken and vegetable pie 30

Pork fillet with tomatoes, cream and Dijon mustard 32

Roast rack of lamb with pinhead oatmeal and cracked black pepper crust,
    with minty Hollandaise sauce 33

Lamb shanks with shallots, raisins and red wine 35

Braised shin of beef with shallots, bacon, mushrooms and red wine 36

Venison fillet stir-fried with spring onions, red peppers, garlic, ginger and sesame oil 37

Baked pasta au gratin 38

Blueberry fool 40

Warm fresh fruit salad in maple syrup with crisp ginger biscuits 41

Rhubarb and orange compote with crisp orange biscuits 43

Rhubarb and orange pistachio meringue pie with ginger pastry 44

Seville orange curd and ginger ice cream with warm dark chocolate sauce 46

Crêpes Suzette 47

Almond lemon tart 49

Apple frangipane tart with lemon pastry 50

Lime water ice with mango and ginger sauce 52

Espresso cream pots 53

Iced coffee cream cake with warm dark chocolate sauce 54

Chocolate and toasted-nut squares 57

Spring starts officially on 21 March, the Vernal Equinox, and as far as I am concerned, continues through April and May. Wherever you live in the UK, this three-month period encompasses a wider variation in weather than any of the other three seasons. It also sees the end of the winter vegetables, which include all types of root, and, in the South, the beginning of the early vegetables including carrots, purple-sprouting broccoli, salad leaves and herbs. In the North of Scotland, early summer is the soonest we have locally grown early vegetables and fruit.

The first part of spring means clearing out – my least favourite part of this time of year – and from the culinary point of view, this is a good time to use up any game left in the freezer. The game terrine recipe (on page 17) is ideal for this as you can put into it any combination of game that happens to be lurking in your freezer.

The menu suggestions for spring (see page 258) are just that: suggestions – you can choose a first course from one menu and a main course from another – but the courses are balanced. Most recipes can be cooked ahead or, at least, prepared well in advance and cooked in minutes. They reflect what is available during the season – rhubarb, for example – and the type of food I enjoy at this time of year. The weather is still changeable: in Skye we often have a snowfall during March, and even in April. We also have torrential rain and howling gales, but the evenings become lighter and summer is around the corner.

Spring is the most beautiful time of the whole year for wild flowers in Skye. The primroses and violets delight us and our hotel guests with their vivid mass of colour, but the leaves on the trees don't start to come out until the end of the first week in May. Spring is the season that shows the most marked difference between North and South. In London the daffodils are usually forgotten when ours are still in bud.

I feel strongly that our eating should be guided by the seasons. In spring you won't find any menus containing asparagus or strawberries. We should wait for them to come into their natural growing season. What you will find are ideas for dishes that are perfect for spring.

Jerusalem artichoke soup with scallops

Jerusalem artichokes taste exquisite, and complement scallops perfectly. The artichokes themselves thicken this soup, and I allow 1 king scallop per person – any more and it would be too filling. It freezes well, or can be made a day or two in advance of when you want to serve it.

Serves 6

3 tbsp extra-virgin olive oil
1 onion, skinned and chopped
1½ lb/700 g peeled Jerusalem artichokes, chopped
1½ pints/900 ml chicken stock
a grating of nutmeg
sea salt and freshly ground black pepper
¼ pint/150 ml double cream, or extra chicken stock
6 large scallops with the corals
2 oz/50 g butter
chopped parsley (optional)

Heat the oil in a saucepan, add the onion and cook over a moderate heat until it is soft and transparent. Add the artichokes and, stirring occasionally, cook for several minutes until they begin to caramelize. Pour in the stock and half-cover the pan. Bring it to the boil, then simmer gently until the biggest piece of artichoke squishes against the side of the pan when you press it with the back of your wooden spoon. This should take about 25 minutes. Liquidize the soup until it is velvety smooth. Pour it back into the pan, taste, and season with nutmeg, salt and pepper. Add the cream, if you are using it, then reheat gently. While the soup is warming through, cook the scallops. Melt the butter in a sauté pan, and when it is foaming, put in the scallops. Sauté them briefly – no more than 30 seconds on each side – then, with scissors, cut each into 4 pieces.

To serve, stir a spoonful of chopped parsley through the soup, then pour it into the bowls and scatter in the scallops.

Roast red pepper, tomato and chilli soup

This is a lovely, warming soup, ideal for a chilly early spring day or evening. Although it looks and tastes comforting, it is light, which allows for a substantial main course and pud. It can be made a couple of days in advance and kept in the fridge.

Serves 6

3 red peppers, halved and seeded
3 tbsp extra-virgin olive oil
2 onions, skinned and chopped
1 lb/450 g vine tomatoes, washed and dried, halved and seeded
1 long red chilli (bird's eye), seeded and finely chopped *or*
½ tsp chilli flakes
1½ pints/900 ml chicken or vegetable stock
sea salt and freshly ground pepper
½ tsp sugar
2 tbsp snipped chives, to garnish
crème fraîche to serve (optional)

Line a baking tray with baking parchment and put the red pepper halves on it, skin side uppermost. Grill until the skin forms black blisters, then put the hot pepper halves into a polythene bag for 10 minutes. The skins should peel off easily. Chop the skinned peppers into chunks.

Heat the oil in a saucepan and sauté the chopped onions until they are soft and transparent. Add the halved tomatoes, the chopped red peppers and the chilli, and cook for 3–5 minutes before adding the stock. Bring it to simmering point, half cover the pan with a lid, and simmer the soup gently for 10 minutes. Allow it to cool, then liquidize it, and sieve it to remove any slivers of tomato skin. Taste, and season accordingly. Reheat to serve, adding the snipped chives just before dishing it up.

If you like, you can spoon a dollop of *crème fraîche* into each serving, and scatter the chives over the top.

Broccoli and lemon soup

When purple sprouting broccoli is available in mid-spring, substitute it for the ordinary broccoli that is available year-round. Whichever variety you use, though, don't waste the stalks: they contain the most flavour. Don't be tempted to use up old broccoli in this soup – the sort that is limp of stalk and yellowing: nothing could mask its past-it flavour.

Serves 6

3 tbsp extra-virgin olive oil
2 onions, skinned and chopped
1–2 cloves of garlic, skinned and chopped (optional)
1 lb/450 g broccoli, trimmed and cut up
1½ pints/900 ml chicken or vegetable stock
sea salt
freshly ground black pepper
a grating of nutmeg
zest of 1 lemon
6 tsp full-fat *crème fraîche*
2 tbsp toasted flaked almonds

Heat the oil in a saucepan and cook the chopped onions until they are soft and beginning to change colour. Add the garlic and the broccoli, and mix them into the onions. Then pour in the stock, season with salt, pepper and a grating of nutmeg, then bring it to a simmer. Half cover the pan, and cook until the thickest piece of stalk is tender. Let the soup cool a little, then liquidize it, with the lemon zest. Pour the soup back into the pan, taste, and adjust the seasoning. To serve, reheat the soup and pour it into bowls. Drop a spoonful of *crème fraîche* on to each and scatter over some toasted almonds.

Blue cheese rarebit on fresh pears

with fried walnuts

You can use any blue cheese you like – except Danish Blue, which always smells of ammonia.

You can peel and core the pears several hours in advance, providing that you brush each pear with lemon juice, put them back together and wrap them in clingfilm, to prevent them discolouring. I like to serve this with a few assorted vinaigrette-dressed salad leaves.

Serves 6

6 ripe pears, ideally Comice, peeled, halved and cored

5 fl oz/150 ml single cream   *for the rarebit*
1 lb/450 g blue cheese
1 tsp balsamic vinegar
3 oz/75 g chopped walnuts, dry-fried to refresh their flavour

Have the pears ready, lightly brushed with lemon juice.

Put the cream into a saucepan and crumble or cut the cheese into it. Over a very gentle heat, let the cheese melt into the cream. Beat it well with the balsamic vinegar. To serve, put 2 pear halves on each plate, spoon the cheese mixture over them and scatter over the walnuts. Serve immediately.

Quails' eggs, avocado and crispy bacon salad

with herb dressing

Serves 6

18 quails' eggs
12 rashers dry-cured streaky bacon, smoked or unsmoked
3 avocados, or more, if they are small and knobbly
assorted salad leaves

for the dressing 1 level tsp sea salt
a good grinding of black pepper
½ teaspoon caster sugar
a good dash of Tabasco
1 tbsp snipped chives
1 tbsp chopped parsley, flat-leaved or curly
1 tbsp chopped basil
10 fl oz/300 ml olive oil
1 tbsp balsamic vinegar

Boil the quails' eggs for 3 minutes until they are hard, then run cold water over them. Crack each around the middle and shell them. Cut each egg in half lengthways. Grill the bacon rashers until they are crisp. Cool them on absorbent kitchen paper, then break them into bits. Halve the avocados, flick out the stones, peel off the skin and slice the flesh into long strips. Put the ingredients for the dressing into a blender and whiz.

To assemble the salad, put clumps of salad leaves on the plates. Arrange the avocado slices and quails' eggs over them. Scatter over the bacon bits then spoon over the dressing and serve.

Potted crab with Melba toast

I was born and spent part of my growing up years near Morecambe Bay, where the shrimps come from. These tiny, slightly peppery-tasting crustaceans are delicious tossed in melted butter flavoured with mace, then packed into pots. But butter with crabmeat is too rich, so instead I use mayonnaise. I hope you will agree that this is an utterly delicious way to eat crab.

Serves 6

1 whole egg and 1 egg yolk *for the mayonnaise*
1 level tsp caster sugar
1 tsp salt
freshly ground black pepper
1 level tsp mustard powder
2 tsp Tabasco
½ pt/300 ml olive oil
juice of 1 lemon

1 lb/450 g equal quantities white and brown crabmeat, mixed well
6 sprigs dill
6 oz/175 g clarified butter (see note below)

First make the mayonnaise: put the egg, the yolk, the sugar, salt, pepper, mustard powder and Tabasco into a food-processor. Whiz, then very gradually add the olive oil, still whizzing. When you have a thick emulsion, add the lemon juice. Stir 2 tablespoons of the mayonnaise into the crabmeat, and divide it evenly between 6 ramekins. Smooth the tops and put a small sprig of dill on each. Carefully pour the clarified butter over the surface of each ramekin, then put them into the fridge until you are ready to serve. I like this served with Melba toast (see page 14), which can be made a day in advance and kept in a sealed polythene bag.

Note: To clarify butter, put it into a saucepan and let it melt over a very low heat without stirring. Then pour out the butter, leaving the curd at the bottom of the pan.

Melba toast

Serves 6

Melba toast is an easy bread accompaniment to so many different dishes, from soups to salads. It can be made several days in advance, providing that you store it in an airtight container.

12 slices from a medium-sliced loaf, either white or brown

Cut the crusts off the bread and toast it. With a sharply serrated bread knife, carefully slice each piece in half so that you have 2 thin slices, toasted on one side. Put the untoasted side under a red-hot grill and leave it until it curls up and is crisply golden brown. Cool, then store in an airtight container or tin.

Lime-marinated fresh and smoked salmon

in *crème fraîche*, dill and cucumber, with pink peppercorns

This dish can be served either as a first course or, if the quantities are doubled, as a main course. You'll need to think ahead: the fish and cucumber are both marinated for several hours – overnight if possible.

Serves 4

8–10 oz/225–275 g filleted raw salmon
zest and juice of 4 limes
1 tsp sea salt
6-in/15-cm piece cucumber, skinned, seeded and diced
2 tbsp white wine vinegar
2 tsp caster sugar
9 fl oz/250 ml full-fat *crème fraîche*
4 oz/110 g smoked salmon, diced
2 tsp pink peppercorns, drained
1–2 tbsp chopped dill
assorted salad leaves

With a very sharp knife, slice the filleted fresh salmon across very thinly, then dice it. Put it into a shallow dish and mix it well with the lime juice and zest, and the salt. In another dish, combine the diced cucumber with the wine vinegar and the caster sugar. Leave the salmon and the cucumber mixtures to marinate for several hours – preferably overnight – stirring once or twice. During this time the fish is 'cooked' by the acid in the lime juice.

To complete the dish, drain the fresh salmon and mix it with the *crème fraîche*. Drain the cucumber and stir it, with the smoked salmon, the pink peppercorns and the dill, into the fresh salmon.

To serve, arrange a few salad leaves on the plates. Spoon over the salmon mixture or, with wetted hands, form it into small mounds on the leaves.

Herb crêpes

with smoked herring roe, cucumber and *crème fraîche*

The crêpe batter can be made up to 2 days in advance, but the crêpes must be made the same day as they are to be eaten. I have recently discovered smoked herring roe: it is Spanish, called avruga, *and is widely available. It is so delicious that I'd rather eat it than caviar.*

Serves 6

for the avruga *filling*
2 x 50 oz/150 g jars *avruga*
½ pint/300 ml full-fat *crème fraîche*
½ cucumber, peeled, seeded and diced
freshly ground black pepper

for the crêpes
4 oz/110 g plain flour
2 large eggs
½ pint/300 ml milk
sea salt
freshly ground black pepper
1 tbsp chopped herbs, including dill, chives and flat-leaf
** parsley (save a sprig of dill to garnish)**
a little butter

Mix together the filling ingredients – you can do this in the morning so that it's ready to put into the crêpes later.

Put all of the ingredients for the crêpes except the butter into a blender and whiz. Leave the batter to stand for a minimum of 30 minutes. If you make it longer in advance, be sure to stir it well before making the crêpes.

Melt a bit of butter the size of your thumbnail in a small frying-pan and pour in a small amount of batter, tipping and tilting the pan so it spreads evenly. Cook for several seconds, then flip it over and cook the other side. Continue until you have used up all the batter. You will have enough for six pancakes. Cool the crêpes on a plastic tray before stacking them. Cover with a cloth or clingfilm.

You can assemble the crêpes 3–4 hours before you need them, provided they are kept in a cool place. To do this, lay a crêpe on a plate, put a spoonful of the filling on half of it, fold over the other half and press lightly to make the filling even. Repeat with a second crêpe, and put the two straight sides together, so that the crêpes form a circle. Lay a sprig of dill down the centre, and cover the plates with clingfilm until just before you eat.

spring first courses

Game terrine with herb jelly

Use any game that you like or have to hand in the terrine. For the jelly, similarly, you can choose any herb but I prefer thyme with game. The jelly can be made weeks in advance, but the terrine will keep for only a couple of days in the fridge.

Serves 6–8

for the marinade

2 medium onions, skinned and very finely chopped
3–4 juniper berries, bashed with the end of a rolling-pin
¼ pint/150 ml red wine
3 tbsp olive oil
zest of 1 orange
pinch of salt
plenty of freshly ground black pepper

1 lb/450 g game meat, off the bone, diced
1 lb/450 g good pork sausages, skinned
12–14 rashers bacon, rind removed
herb jelly (page 18)

Put all the ingredients for the marinade into a small saucepan and simmer gently for 1 minute. Pour it into a bowl and leave it to cool completely. Put the game meat and the sausages into the marinade and mix together thoroughly with your hands. Leave to marinate for 6–8 hours minimum, or overnight.

Preheat the oven to 350°F/180°C/Gas Mark 4. Line a loaf or terrine tin with foil. Stretch the bacon rashers with a knife and use them to line the tin. Pack in the game mixture, cover it with foil, and put the terrine into a roasting tin. Pour water into the tin to a depth of 2 inches/5 cm, to make a bain marie, and put the tin into the oven to bake for 2 hours. Push a skewer or a sharp knife into the centre of the terrine: if the juices run pink, return the terrine to the oven for another 15–30 minutes. The cooked juices should run clear. Take it out and put a weight on top – I use a large tin of tomatoes or similar. Leave it to cool completely, then remove the weight and store the terrine in the fridge until you need it. To serve, turn it out and peel off the foil. Put a slice on each plate with some herb jelly (see page 18).

herb jelly

Makes 4 lb/1.8 kg

1 lb/450 g cooking apples
1 lb/450 g good eating apples
4 x 4-in/10-cm sprigs thyme
¼ pint/150 ml white wine vinegar
1 lb/450 g granulated or preserving sugar to each 1 pint/600 ml liquid

Wash the apples well and chop them into chunks, skin, core and all. Put them into a large saucepan with the thyme, 3 pints/1.7 litres water and the vinegar. Cover the pan with its lid and simmer the contents until the pieces of apple are mushy. Strain the contents of the pan through a jelly bag, or through a sieve lined with a new J-cloth or a large piece of muslin. Don't squeeze the contents of the bag or the jelly will be cloudy. Measure the juice and put it back into the washed-out saucepan with the sugar. Over a moderate heat stir until the sugar has dissolved, then boil fast. After 10 minutes, pull the pan off the heat, drip some of the hot liquid on to a saucer, and leave it to get completely cold. Push the dribble of jelly with your finger and if it has reached setting point it will wrinkle. If it is still runny put the pan back on to the heat and boil it fast for a further 5 minutes. Retest it for a set. Allow it to cool a little, then pour it into sterilized warmed jars, cover each with a waxed paper disc, and seal with Cellophane. Store the jars in a cool cupboard or, ideally, a larder.

Sautéed chicken livers

with garlic, apples and balsamic vinegar

If you prepare this in advance, rub out a bowl with olive oil before you put the picked-over chicken livers into it – that way you won't get a blood line on the bowl that takes ages to wash up afterwards.

Serves 6

3 good eating apples
3 tbsp extra-virgin olive oil
2 cloves garlic, skinned and very finely chopped
2 lb/900 g fresh chicken livers, weighed and trimmed of green bits
1 tbsp balsamic vinegar
sea salt
freshly ground black pepper
assorted salad leaves

Peel, core and slice the apples ¼-in/0.5-cm thick. (If you do this in advance, dip them in lemon juice to prevent them discolouring.) Heat the oil in a large sauté pan and add the apples and the garlic. Cook for a couple of minutes, then gently spoon them on to a warm dish and add the chicken livers to the pan. Sauté them, stirring so that they firm up and cook evenly. Put the apples and garlic back into the pan, with the livers, and add the balsamic vinegar. Stir it in carefully, and season with salt and pepper. Spoon the livers with the apples and garlic over or beside the salad leaves.

Spicy hummus with carrot sticks

Serves 6

I love hummus, but this version makes it much more interesting. I use canned chickpeas, well drained. If you prefer dried, soak them overnight then simmer them until they are soft.

2 x 14 oz/400 g cans chickpeas
6 tbsp extra-virgin olive oil
3 red onions, skinned and very finely chopped
2 cloves garlic, skinned and finely chopped
½ tsp cumin seeds
½ tsp powdered cinnamon
½ tsp ground ginger
2 bashed cardamom pods
1 tsp Tabasco
4 tomatoes, skinned, seeded and diced
sea salt
freshly ground black pepper
2 tbsp lemon juice
1 tbsp chopped parsley
carrots, peeled and cut into fat julienne strips

Put the drained chickpeas into a food-processor and whiz to a rough purée. Heat the olive oil in a sauté pan and add the onions. Cook over a moderate heat until they are soft, then add the garlic and cook for a few seconds. Add the spices, Tabasco, tomatoes and puréed chickpeas. Season well with salt and pepper, then cook, stirring carefully, for another 10 minutes. Mix in the lemon juice. Let the contents of the pan cool, then stir in the parsley.

Scrape this delicious hummus into a bowl, and serve it with fat strips of carrot – and some salad leaves too, if you like.

spring first courses

Marinated grilled aubergine slices

with tomato and chilli sauce

This is one of my favourite ways to eat aubergines. If you prefer you can serve the aubergine slices warm from the grill, without marinating them in olive oil, but that involves more kitchen action just before supper than if you serve them cold. As aubergines vary so much in size, you will have to judge when you buy them how many you will need. You can make the sauce a couple of days ahead, but keep it in the fridge.

Serves 6

24 lengthways slices aubergine, ¼ in/½ cm thick
extra-virgin olive oil
a few sprigs thyme
sea salt
freshly ground black pepper

3 tbsp extra-virgin olive oil *for the sauce*
2 onions, skinned and finely chopped
2 sticks celery, strings removed and thinly sliced
1–2 cloves garlic, skinned and finely chopped
1 long red chilli, seeded and chopped
2 x 14 oz/400 g tins chopped tomatoes
½ tsp sugar
½ tsp (or more) sea salt
a good grinding of black pepper
2 tbsp chopped parsley

Brush each aubergine slice on both sides with olive oil. Line a baking tray with foil and put the first batch of slices on to it. Grill until they are brown – don't let them burn. Turn them over with a fish-slice and grill on the other side. Lay them in a large dish, and repeat with the rest of the slices. When they are all in the dish, trickle extra-virgin olive oil over them, and lay the sprigs of thyme among them. Scatter over some salt, and add a good grinding of black pepper.

Now make the sauce: heat the olive oil in a saucepan and cook the onions and celery until the onions are soft and beginning to turn colour. Then add the garlic, the chilli, and the tomatoes. Stir in the sugar and seasoning, and let the sauce simmer gently for 10–15 minutes.

I like to serve the sauce warm, but you can just as well serve it at room temperature. Just before eating stir the chopped parsley through the sauce.

To serve, put 3 aubergine slices on each plate – a few are left over for second helpings – and either pass the sauce separately in a bowl, or dollop it on to the plates.

Spaghetti with white crabmeat,

olive oil, garlic, chilli and parsley

This simple but delicious pasta dish needs only a green salad to accompany it. The garlic and chilli can be prepared several hours in advance, providing that they are mixed together and covered with olive oil. You can chop the parsley ahead of time too: cover it with clingfilm, and leave it in the fridge. Unusually for me this recipe uses just white crabmeat: although the brown has more flavour, it makes the end result mushy.

Serves 6

1 lb/450 g spaghetti
1–2 cloves garlic, skinned and very finely chopped
1 bird's eye or medium-strength chilli, halved, seeded and finely chopped
4–5 tbsp extra-virgin olive oil
1½ lb/700 g white crabmeat, picked over to remove all shell
3 oz/75 g parsley, flat leaf if possible, chopped
freshly ground black pepper
½ tsp sea salt

Cook the spaghetti in a good quantity of boiling salted water for 6–7 minutes. Drain, and immediately mix in the garlic, chilli and olive oil. Put in the crabmeat, parsley, pepper and salt – you do need the salt to enhance the taste of the crab. Mix everything together thoroughly to allow the crabmeat to warm through. Serve as soon as you can.

Salmon fillets with watercress and shallot sauce

Serves 4

for the
watercress and
shallot sauce

4 shallots, skinned and very finely chopped
½ stick celery, strings removed and thinly sliced
2 oz/50 g butter
½ pint/300 ml chicken stock
3 oz/75 g watercress
5 fl oz/150 ml single cream
½ tsp sugar
sea salt
freshly ground black pepper

4 x 6 oz/175 g pieces filleted salmon
6 oz/175 g butter
sea salt
freshly ground black pepper

To make the sauce, sauté the shallots and the celery in the butter for 3–4 minutes, then pour in the stock and simmer until the liquid has reduced by half. Put the contents of the saucepan into a blender and whiz, gradually adding the watercress and the cream. Add the sugar and taste, then adjust the seasoning if necessary. You can reheat the sauce gently, but do not let it boil. Serve it spooned beside each helping of salmon.

To cook the salmon I find that there is no better way than the method John Tovey taught me many years ago. Preheat the oven to 420°F/220°C/Gas Mark 7. Lay the fish on a buttered baking tray, place on each piece about 1 oz/25 g of butter and season with sea salt and black pepper. Put it into the oven for 5 minutes. (Allow a further minute in the oven for 8 pieces of fish, and increase the cooking time by a minute for any more.)

Hot-smoked salmon fishcakes

with lime and shallot sauce

Everyone loves a crispy fishcake and these make a perfect main course alone, but they are dressed up here with the lime and shallot sauce.

The fishcakes freeze well for up to 2 weeks, but no longer because the salmon starts to taste oily. Thaw frozen fishcakes in a single layer: it takes 2–3 hours at room temperature. You can make the sauce several hours ahead too, if you like.

Serves 6

1 lb/450 g hot-smoked salmon, flaked
1 lb/450 g mashed potato
2 oz/50 g butter
2 tbsp snipped chives
2 level tbsp chopped fresh parsley
sea salt
freshly ground black pepper
2 level tbsp plain flour
2 beaten eggs
4 oz/110 g dry breadcrumbs

3 tbsp extra-virgin olive oil
8 banana shallots or 12 smaller ones, skinned and finely chopped
1 pint/600 ml chicken or vegetable stock
zest and juice of 3 limes
¾ pint/450 ml double cream
sea salt
freshly ground black pepper

for the lime and shallot sauce

Mix together the salmon, the potato, mashed with half of the butter, the chives and the parsley. Season, then shape the mixture into 12 fat cakes 1½ in/3 cm across. Dip them first into the flour, then into the egg and finally the breadcrumbs. Chill for 15 minutes.

Preheat the oven to 475°F/240°C/Gas Mark 9. Melt the remaining butter, brush it all over the fishcakes and bake them for 20–25 minutes or until they are golden brown. If you prefer, omit the butter at this stage, and shallow fry the fishcakes in oil.

The sauce is cooked quickest in a wide sauté pan – the stock takes less time to reduce. Heat the olive oil and put in the chopped shallots. Sauté over a moderate heat until they are very soft, then add the stock and let it bubble until it has reduced to almost nothing. Add the lime zest and juice, and finally the cream. Mix well, let it come to the boil, just, and season.

Baked marinated tuna steaks

with Parmesan pasta

This is a splendid main course, satisfying both in taste and texture. I have to thank our second daughter, Isabella, for the idea – she put together the combination of ingredients, and serves the pasta warm, not hot.

Serves 6

6 x 6 oz/175 g tuna steaks
3 tbsp harissa – hot chilli paste
6 tbsp olive oil

12 oz/350 g short pasta, such as penne   *for the pasta*
3 red onions, skinned and thinly sliced
3 tbsp olive oil
1 tbsp capers, preserved in olive oil
1 tbsp chopped coriander
2 oz/50 g freshly grated Parmesan
freshly grated black pepper

Put the tuna steaks into a wide dish and smear each with the harissa. Spoon over the olive oil, cover, and leave in a cool place for several hours, or overnight.

To start the pasta sauce, preheat the oven to 350°F/180°C/Gas Mark 4. Stir the onions in 1 tablespoon of the olive oil, then tip them on to a baking tray lined with baking parchment. Put them in the oven and roast until they are turning golden at the edges.

When you wish to cook the tuna steaks, preheat the oven to 350°F/ 180°C/Gas Mark 4. Put the tuna steaks between 2 sheets of baking parchment on a baking tray, and put them in the oven for 15–20 minutes – exactly how long depends on the thickness of the steaks. Test to see if they are cooked by gently pulling apart the centre of one steak, using 2 forks. If it still looks a bit raw for your liking, replace the paper and put the dish back into the oven for another 5 minutes.

Meanwhile, bring to the boil a saucepan of salted water and cook the pasta until it is *al dente*. Drain it and mix it with the remaining olive oil, the onion, capers and coriander. Just before dishing up, spoon through the Parmesan and season well with pepper. Spoon some pasta on to each warmed plate, and put a tuna steak on top.

Spicy red fish stew

This was a happy invention for supper one evening last spring. You can make the sauce the day before, and prepare the fish, too. When you reheat the sauce, just slip the prepared fish into it to cook – it takes only a few minutes. If you like, you can serve a green vegetable with it, but I think it is unnecessary.

Serves 6

3 red peppers
4–5 tbsp extra-virgin olive oil
6 banana shallots, or 12 smaller ones, skinned and chopped
1–2 cloves garlic, skinned and finely chopped
2 x 14 oz/400 g tins chopped tomatoes
1–2 bird's eye chillies, seeded and chopped, *or*
   1 rounded tsp dried chilli flakes
sea salt
finely grated zest of 2 limes
1 tbsp chopped coriander
2½ lb/1.2 kg cod, skinned, filleted and cut into 1-in/2-cm chunks

Cut each pepper in half and put them, skin side uppermost, on a baking tray under a red-hot grill. Leave them until black blisters form, then put them into a polythene bag for 10 minutes. The skin should then peel off easily. Chop the skinned peppers.

Meanwhile, heat the olive oil in a large sauté pan and cook the shallots until they are very soft. Stir in the garlic and the tomatoes. Add the chilli, and the red peppers. Season with salt, and let the sauce simmer gently for 10–15 minutes. Stir in the lime zest, and the coriander, then add the fish and simmer gently till it turns opaque – this should take no longer than 5 minutes. Serve in soup plates or bowls with warm bread or garlic bread as an accompaniment.

Smoked haddock creamy stew

with shallots, saffron and baby spinach

*This is a heavenly dish. I don't think you need anything else to eat with it –
although bread or even plain boiled potatoes would go well. Don't stint on
the cream: accompany it with a leafy salad and finish with fresh fruit. You can
make this a day before you want to eat it – keep it in a bowl in the fridge –
or just chop and sauté the shallots beforehand if you wish.*

Serves 6

3 tbsp extra-virgin olive oil
8–10 shallots, depending on their size, skinned and finely chopped
2–2½ lb/900 g – 1.2 kg filleted undyed smoked haddock, cut into 1½-in/4-cm chunks
1 pint/600 ml double cream
½ tsp saffron strands
plenty of freshly ground black pepper
4 oz/110 g baby spinach leaves

Heat the olive oil in a large sauté pan and cook the shallots until they
are soft. Add the fish, the cream and the saffron, and heat gently
until the cream is simmering. The fish will take about 3 minutes to
cook. Season with pepper – the smoked haddock should be
sufficiently salty – and put in the spinach: it will be a high mound, but
cover the pan with a lid, and it will wilt quickly. When it has wilted,
combine it evenly, but carefully so as not to break up the pieces of
fish more than you can help, with the contents of the sauté pan. To
serve, ladle into warmed bowls.

Chicken and vegetable pie

This is a perfect main course for comfort eating at any time, but especially on a cold spring day when impatience for warmer weather sets in. Everything – including the vegetables – is in it so you can serve it on its own. You could cover it with puff pastry if you prefer, but I like shortcrust pastry for this pie. You can prepare the pie in advance, the day before, and bake it later.

Serves 6

8 banana shallots, or 12 smaller ones, skinned and sliced
2 carrots, peeled and diced thumbnail size
3 leeks, trimmed, washed and thinly sliced
4 parsnips, peeled and diced thumbnail size
6 celery sticks, strings removed and sliced, *or* 3 extra leeks
2 tbsp olive oil
sea salt
freshly ground black pepper
1 x 3 lb/1.35 kg chicken, preferably organic
2 oz/50 g cold butter, cut into small dice
2 fairly level tbsp plain flour
8 oz/225 g frozen peas, thawed
sprig of thyme
2 lb/900 g shortcrust pastry
1 egg, beaten

Preheat the oven to 375°F/190°C/Gas Mark 5, and have ready a 5-pint/2-litre pie dish.

In a bowl mix together the prepared vegetables, apart from the peas, and stir in the olive oil thoroughly. Add 1 teaspoon salt and plenty of black pepper. Put the vegetables into a heavy casserole or roasting tin, and push the chicken, breast side down, among them. Cover it with a lid, and put it into the oven for 40 minutes. Then turn the chicken breast side up and roast without the lid for a further 35–40 minutes. Take it out and let it cool. If you wish to cook the pie now, turn the oven up to 400°F/200°C/Gas Mark 6.

Lift the chicken out of the casserole or tin and cut all the meat from the bones. Throw away all the skin and gristle but keep the bones for making chicken stock. Dice the meat and put it into a large bowl. With a slotted spoon lift all the vegetables out of the roasting tin or casserole, leaving behind the cooking juices, and put them into the bowl with the chicken. In a food-processor, whiz the butter, hard from the fridge, with the flour until it resembles crumbs. Heat the juices in the roasting tin or casserole, then whisk in the butter-and-flour crumbs, until the sauce is thick and bubbling – scraping any chicken and vegetable bits off the bottom of the pan. If it seems too thick, thin it with a little milk; the sauce should be the consistency of pouring cream. Make sure the sauce bubbles well after you have added any milk. Let the sauce cool, stirring from time to time to prevent a skin forming, then stir it into the vegetables and chicken. Now add the thawed peas and the thyme. Put the mixture into the pie dish.

Roll out the pastry and use it to cover the dish, dampening the edge of the dish with water or egg, and crimping the pastry around the edges – I use the tines of a fork to do this. Decorate, if you like, with pastry roses. Brush with beaten egg, then cut 3 slashes in the top of the pie. Put it into the oven for 40–45 minutes, or until the pastry is golden brown. Keep the pie warm in a cool oven until you are ready to serve it. If the pastry browns early in the cooking time, cover it with a sheet of baking parchment.

Pork fillet with tomatoes, cream

and Dijon mustard

This is a simple but delicious dish. The pork fillet marinates in soy sauce, which might sound odd – the brand you use makes all the difference to the recipe. The best widely available make is Kikkoman's, but many towns and cities in the UK have a Chinese supermarket where you will find the best of all soy sauces, Kicap Manis. Recently at a demonstration here at Kinloch a guest asked me if I had ever tried marinating salmon in Kicap Manis. I haven't – yet – but apparently it's wonderful!

Serves 6

3 x 1½ lb/700 g pork fillets
6 tbsp soy sauce
3 tbsp extra-virgin olive oil
½ pint/300 ml double cream
1 tbsp Dijon mustard
pepper
6 vine tomatoes, skinned, seeded and sliced into thick strips

Slice each pork fillet lengthways but not right through. Spread them out and put them between 2 sheets of baking parchment or cling-film. Bash, with a rolling pin, until the meat is well flattened. Cut each piece in half, then put them on to a large flat dish and spoon over the soy sauce. Leave overnight to marinate.

Heat the oil in a sauté pan and brown each piece of pork, which will cook it through. Put the meat on to a large warmed dish. Add the cream, mustard and pepper to the sauté pan and let it bubble. Replace the browned pieces of pork, and add the tomatoes. Let it simmer gently for a minute or two, to heat through. Serve, if you like, with potatoes roasted in olive oil with rosemary, and a green vegetable.

Roast rack of lamb with pinhead oatmeal

and cracked black pepper crust with minty Hollandaise sauce

You should be able to buy pinhead oatmeal from a health-food shop. The reduced and cooled white wine vinegar needed for the sauce can be made in advance and kept in a screw-top jar in the fridge.

Serves 6

3 racks of lamb
6 tbsp pinhead oatmeal
approximately 1 tsp sea salt
about 30 twists of black pepper from the mill

¼ pint/150 ml white wine vinegar
6–8 peppercorns
a bay leaf
a few crushed parsley stalks
½ onion
3 large egg yolks
6–8 oz/175–225 g butter
1 tbsp chopped mint – apple mint if possible

for the minty Hollandaise sauce

First make the sauce. Put the wine vinegar into a small saucepan with the peppercorns, bay leaf, parsley stalks and the half-onion, and simmer until it has reduced by half. Leave it to get cold, then strain it. Put the egg yolks into a Pyrex bowl over a saucepan of simmering water about 2 in/5 cm deep. Whisk the flavoured wine vinegar into the yolks, then add the butter, about 1 oz/25 g at a time. Stir with the whisk until it has melted before adding another piece. Keep the water beneath the bowl at a gentle simmer as you stir in the butter pieces. You should end up with a thick sauce. Take the bowl off the heat and stir in the chopped mint. This sauce will keep its heat and can be made an hour before serving. Keep it in a warm place, but not over direct heat.

Preheat the oven to 400°F/200°C/Gas Mark 6. Lay a sheet of baking parchment in a roasting tin – this will make washing-up much easier.

Now either cut the fat and skin from the racks – easy with a sharp knife – or, if you like to eat fat, leave it on but score it in lines across then diagonally. Mix together the oatmeal, salt and pepper, then scatter it over the racks. Roast the lamb for 20–25 minutes if you like the meat rare. As I like it cooked right through – unfashionable, I know – I leave them for 1 hour, covered with a piece of baking parchment for the first 30 minutes to stop the oatmeal scorching. Also, if you leave on the fat, a lengthy cooking time allows it to crisp up and much of it melts into the meat. Delicious!

To serve the lamb, you can either cut each rack in half and serve it as it is, with the sauce, or you can cut between each bone and arrange 3 chops per person on each warmed plate. You could buy some of those white paper frills, specially made to cover the ends of the bones, but I confess I have never done this!

Lamb shanks with shallots, raisins and red wine

The long slow cooking of the meat results in a delicious sweetness of flavour that is well complemented by the shallots, raisins and wine. A good mixed-leaf salad and baked jacket potatoes are all that is needed to accompany it. If the lamb shanks are small, allow 1 per person. You can cook the casserole the day before you want to eat it, and reheat it.

Serves 6

3 tbsp extra-virgin olive oil
3 or 6 lamb shanks, depending on size
1½ lb/700 g banana shallots, skinned and halved, or smaller ones skinned and left whole
2 cloves garlic, skinned and finely chopped (optional)
4 oz/110 g raisins, preferably Lexia
½ pint/300 ml good red wine
3 tsp balsamic vinegar
sea salt
freshly ground black pepper

Preheat the oven to 300°F/150°C/Gas Mark 2.

Heat the oil in a heavy casserole that has a lid, and brown each lamb shank well on all sides. Remove the shanks and keep them warm, then add the shallots to the casserole. Sauté them over a moderate heat for several minutes until they are turning golden. Then add the garlic and cook for a further minute before adding the raisins, wine, balsamic vinegar, a seasoning of salt and plenty of pepper. Bring the liquid to the boil, then replace the shanks in the casserole. Let the liquid bubble again before covering the casserole with its lid, and put it into the oven for 2 hours. Then lower the temperature to 250°F/100°C/Gas Mark 1 and cook for another hour. When it is ready the meat should fall off the bone.

If you cooked the lamb the day before, reheat it with the lid on, in a moderate oven – 350°F/180°C/Gas Mark 4 – to the point where the liquid just bubbles around the meat for 10–15 minutes.

Braised shin of beef

with shallots, bacon, mushrooms and red wine

You can make this with rump steak if you prefer, but I like the rich, gelatinous texture of shin, which cooks up into a glossy-sauced dish, full of flavour. As with all stews and casseroles, this benefits from being made in advance, then kept in the fridge or a cold larder. (You could freeze it, but for a limited length of time – 4–6 weeks; after this time the bacon will start to taste rancid.)

Serves 6

12 tbsp olive oil

12 banana shallots, skinned and halved lengthways, or 18 smaller ones, left whole

1 lb/450 g open mushrooms, wiped and sliced or quartered

3 lb/1.35 kg trimmed shin of beef, cut into 2-in/5-cm chunks

2 rashers unsmoked bacon, cut into thin strips

1 tbsp flour

1½ pints/900 ml red wine and beef or vegetable stock mixed – I leave the ratio up to you!

sea salt

freshly ground black pepper

a grating of nutmeg

Preheat the oven to 300°F/150°C/Gas Mark 2.

Heat 4 tablespoons of the olive oil in a heavy casserole and sauté the shallots, turning them until they are golden all over. Scoop them into a warmed dish, and set aside. In the same casserole sauté the mushrooms in the remaining olive oil, in three batches, until they are almost crisp. Add the mushrooms to the shallots and then brown the pieces of beef, a few at a time. Put them in the dish with the shallots and mushrooms. Add the bacon and cook for a couple of minutes, then stir in the flour. Cook again for a couple of minutes, then pour in the wine and stock mixture, stirring continuously until the sauce bubbles. Replace the shallots and the beef in the casserole, and add the mushrooms. Season with salt, black pepper, and a grating of nutmeg, bring the liquid back to bubbling point, cover the casserole with its lid and put it into the oven for 2½ hours. Then stick a fork into a bit of meat: it should feel quite tender. If it doesn't, replace the lid, and continue to cook for a further 30 minutes. It will keep warm without spoiling for up to an hour. I like to serve this with well-mashed potatoes, and a mixed-leaf salad, dressed with vinaigrette, on the side.

Venison fillet stir-fried with spring onions,

red peppers, garlic, ginger and sesame oil

All the ingredients for this recipe can be prepared in advance. The
actual cooking takes minutes.

Serves 6

3 tbsp extra-virgin olive oil

2½ lb/1.2 kg venison fillet, sliced into strips 2-in/3-cm long, no thicker than a little finger

2 red peppers, halved, seeded and thinly sliced into strips

about 12 spring onions, trimmed, halved, then sliced lengthways into 3

1 tsp finely chopped or grated ginger

1–2 fat cloves garlic, skinned and finely chopped

½ tsp dried chilli flakes

1 tbsp sesame oil

2 tbsp dark soya sauce

3–4 tbsp chopped coriander

Heat the olive oil in a wok or a large sauté pan until it is smoking.
Cook the venison strips, in batches, until they are brown, then scoop
them into a warmed bowl. When all the meat is browned, lower the
heat slightly, and add the red peppers, the spring onions, the ginger
and garlic to the wok or pan. Stir-fry until the pepper softens. Add the
chilli flakes and the sesame oil, replace the browned venison strips,
the soya sauce and coriander and cook everything together for a
minute. Serve on warmed plates.

Basmati rice is the best accompaniment, if you feel you need
something.

Baked pasta au gratin

This is the perfect main course: it can be made entirely in advance and popped in the oven 30–40 minutes before you eat. All that is needed to go with it is a mixed-leaf salad.

Beware: I use harissa to spice up this sauce, and the result is fairly hot. Harissa is widely available from delicatessens and even large supermarkets. If you can't find it, use 2 scant teaspoons dried chilli, though this is a poor substitute for the depth of taste you would get from harissa.

Serves 6

for the tomato sauce

18 oz/500 g short pasta, such as bows or shells
2 onions, skinned and chopped
4 tbsp extra-virgin olive oil
2 cloves garlic, skinned and finely chopped
2 sticks celery, trimmed and chopped
2 x 14 oz/400 g tins chopped tomatoes
1 level tbsp harissa
salt
freshly ground black pepper

for the cheese sauce

2 oz/50 g butter
2 scant tbsp flour
1¼ pints/725 ml milk
1 tsp Dijon mustard
1 tsp balsamic vinegar
6 oz/175 g Parmesan, grated
salt
freshly ground black pepper

First make the tomato sauce. In a saucepan, sauté the chopped onions in the olive oil until they are very soft and just beginning to turn golden at the edges. At this point add the garlic and celery and cook for a further 5 minutes. Stir in the chopped tomatoes and the harissa. Bring the sauce to simmering point and simmer very gently, with the pan half covered, for 10 minutes. Taste, and season with salt and pepper.

Meanwhile, make the cheese sauce. Melt the butter in another saucepan, stir in the flour and let this mixture cook for half a minute. Then gradually add the milk, stirring briskly until you have a smooth sauce. Keep stirring until it comes to the boil. Draw the pan off the heat and stir in the mustard and vinegar (both of which will underline the cheese flavour), and half of the grated Parmesan. Season with salt and pepper, and cover the surface of the sauce with a dampened, wrung-out piece of greaseproof paper to prevent a skin forming.

Cook the pasta in plenty of boiling salted water. When you can stick a (clean) thumbnail into a piece of pasta and it is *al dente* (still with a bit of bite), drain it well and mix it with the tomato sauce. Oil an ovenproof dish and pour the tomatoey pasta into it. Cover the pasta with the cheese sauce, and sprinkle the remaining Parmesan over the top. Bake in a moderate oven, 350°F/180°C/Gas Mark 4, for about 30 minutes, until the cheese is bubbling and golden.

Blueberry fool

Well, I love blueberries raw, and I love them cooked. When they are cooked, they lose their bloom, and the colour and flavour sharpen. You have to sweeten them. Not only do they taste delicious, they are full of antioxidants and very good for us.

Serves 6

1½ lb/700 g blueberries
4 tbsp water
3 large egg whites
a pinch of salt
3 oz/75 g icing sugar, sieved
½ pint/300 ml double cream, whipped into soft peaks

Put the blueberries into a saucepan with the water. Cover the pan with a lid, and cook over a moderate heat until the berries are soft. Take them off the heat, purée them and then sieve them. Leave to cool. Whisk the egg whites with a pinch of salt until they are fairly stiff. Then whisk in the sieved icing sugar, a spoonful at a time, until it is all incorporated. Fold the cooled blueberry purée into the whipped cream, then fold in the stiff meringue, leaving the fool streaky, which looks attractive. Spoon the fool into serving glasses.

If you like, you can cook some extra blueberries, and put a spoonful at the bottom of each glass with the fool on top.

Warm fresh fruit salad in maple syrup

with crisp ginger biscuits

The fruit can be prepared up to a day ahead, then covered closely with cling-film. I love both the ginger and the cardamom in this recipe, but beware of using too much cardamom – it is a highly aromatic spice. Leave out the ginger if you don't like it. Leftovers are very good at breakfast time.

Serves 6

1 pineapple
4 pears – preferably Conference
3 good eating apples – Cox's are ideal
juice of 1 lemon
1 lb/450 g grapes
3 pink grapefruit
1 pint/600 ml best maple syrup
3–6 pieces stem ginger, chopped, to taste
3 bashed cardamom seeds

Peel the pineapple, quarter it lengthwise, then slice off the core from each piece. Cut each quarter into neat chunks.

Peel and core the pears and apples, then cut them into neat slices or chunks. Put them into a bowl and mix them thoroughly with the lemon juice. Press clingfilm over the surface. Halve the grapes and remove any seeds. With a serrated knife cut the skin from the grape-fruit and cut in towards the middle of each fruit, between the membrane. Collect the juice and pithless segments in a bowl.

Pour the maple syrup into a large sauté pan and add the ginger and cardamom. Put in the apples and pears, then simmer gently for a couple of minutes. Add the rest of the fruit, turning it carefully in the maple syrup, so that it doesn't break up, as it cooks gently. The inevitable casualty if the fruit salad remains hot for any length of time is the grapefruit, but its flavour within the dish is wonderful. Pour the fruit into a heatproof serving bowl and keep it warm in a low oven until you are ready to serve it.

ginger biscuits

Makes 12–16

4 oz/110 g butter
2 oz/50 g caster sugar
4 oz/110 g self-raising flour
2 rounded tsp ground ginger

Preheat the oven to 350°F/180°C/Gas Mark 4.

Beat together the butter and sugar until it is light in colour and soft in texture. Sieve in the flour and ground ginger, a little at a time, beating well until it is all incorporated and you have a stiff dough. Dust the palms of your hands with a little flour, then take pieces of dough about the size of a walnut and roll them into balls. Put them on to a baking tray – no need to butter it – spaced well apart. Flatten each with a fork. Bake for 10–15 minutes, or until the biscuits are light golden brown. When they are ready, they should still feel softish, but they will firm up as they cool. Once they are out of the oven, leave them on the baking tray for a minute or two, then lift them off with a palette knife and leave them on a wire cooling rack. Store them in an airtight container.

spring puddings

Rhubarb and orange compote

with crisp orange biscuits

Rhubarb is so good with orange, ginger and, to a slightly lesser extent, cinnamon. If you, like me, love ginger, add some chopped preserved ginger to the compote.

Serves 6

2 lb/900 g trimmed rhubarb, cut into 1½-in/4-cm chunks
6 oz/175 g soft light brown sugar
finely grated zest and juice of 2 oranges

Preheat the oven to 350°F/180°C/Gas Mark 4.

Put all the above ingredients into an ovenproof dish with a lid, cover it, and bake until the rhubarb is tender, but not collapsed, 30–40 minutes.

crisp orange biscuits

Makes 10–12 biscuits

4 oz/110 g self-raising flour
2¼ oz/55 g caster sugar, plus a little extra
3 oz/75 g butter, diced
finely grated zest of 1 orange
1 large egg yolk
1 egg white
caster sugar

Preheat the oven to 350°F/180°C/Gas Mark 4. Put the flour, sugar and butter into a food-processor. Whiz until the mixture is crumb-like, then add the orange zest and the egg yolk. Whiz until the dough forms a ball. Take it out of the food-processor and roll it out ¼ in/ 0.5 cm thick. Cut it into 2-in/5-cm rounds and put them on to a lightly buttered or oiled baking tray. Brush each with egg white and sprinkle a small amount of caster sugar on top. Bake for 10–12 minutes. Take the biscuits out of the oven and let them cool for a minute. Lift them on to a wire cooling rack, using a palette knife. When cold, store in an airtight container.

Rhubarb and orange pistachio meringue pie

with ginger pastry

This pie combines rhubarb, orange and ginger in a crisp pastry base with a marshmallow meringue on top. You can make the pastry up to a week in advance, providing you keep it in an airtight container or freeze it. The orange and rhubarb purée for the filling can also be made early and frozen, or kept in the fridge for up to three days.

Serves 6–8

for the pastry
4 oz/110 g butter, cut into bits
6 oz/175 g plain flour
2 tsp ground ginger
1 oz/25 g icing sugar

for the filling
2 lb/900 g rhubarb, trimmed and cut into chunks
grated zest and juice of 1 orange
4–6 oz/110–175 g soft brown sugar, to taste
2 large eggs
2 large egg yolks – keep the whites to make up the number needed for the meringue top

for the meringue
4 large egg whites
a pinch of salt
8 oz/225 g icing sugar, sieved
3 oz/75 g shelled pistachio nuts – not salted

Preheat the oven to 350°F/180°C/Gas Mark 4.

Put the pastry ingredients into a processor and whiz to a crumb-like consistency. Pat and press this mixture firmly around the sides and base of an 9-in/23-cm loose-bottomed flan tin or ceramic flan dish. Put it into the fridge for 1 hour, then bake for 20 minutes: the pastry should be biscuit-coloured. If not, put it back for another 5 minutes.

Meanwhile, put the rhubarb into a saucepan with the orange zest and juice and the sugar, and cook over a moderate heat until the rhubarb is soft, 20–25 minutes. Let it cool, then purée it in the food-processor.

Beat together the eggs and the yolks, then beat them thoroughly into the rhubarb and orange purée. Pour this into the pastry case and return it to the oven until the filling is just set in the middle. After 15 minutes shake the flan dish: if it wobbles in the centre it needs a few more minutes in the oven. When it is ready, take it out and let it cool. Don't turn off the oven.

Put the egg whites and salt into a Pyrex bowl over a saucepan of simmering water, and whisk, gradually adding the sieved icing sugar, until the meringue is very thick. Take the bowl off the heat and continue to whisk for a couple of minutes. Quickly fold in the pistachio nuts and spoon the meringue over the pie, taking it right over the edges of the pastry. Bake for just long enough to turn the top of the meringue light golden – 12–15 minutes – and serve cold or warm, with whipped cream.

Seville orange curd and ginger ice cream

with warm dark chocolate sauce

Serves 6

This is a perfect pud for early spring. It makes the most of Seville oranges in their all-too-brief season.

for the curd

4 oz/110 g butter, cut into pieces
4 oz/ 110 g sugar, caster or granulated
1 large whole egg, beaten well with 2 yolks – save the whites for the ice cream
finely grated zest and juice of 4 Seville oranges

for the ice cream

3 large egg whites
a pinch of salt
3 oz/75 g icing sugar, sieved
6 pieces preserved ginger, drained and chopped
½ pint/300 ml double cream, whipped

1 quantity Warm Dark Chocolate Sauce (see page 56)

Put all the curd ingredients into a heatproof bowl, and set it over a saucepan of gently simmering water. Stir until the sugar dissolves and the butter melts. The curd will then gradually thicken – you need only give it the occasional stir during this time. Let it cool, pot it and store it in the fridge. It will keep there safely for a week.

To make the ice cream, whisk the egg whites with the salt until they are fairly stiff, then whisk in the icing sugar, a spoonful at a time, whisking continuously until it is all incorporated. With a large metal spoon, fold in the chopped ginger, the whipped cream and the Seville orange curd. Scrape it into a polythene container with a lid, and freeze.

Take the ice cream out of the freezer at least 30 minutes before serving – it is better slightly softened than rock-solid from the freezer. Serve with the Warm Dark Chocolate Sauce.

spring puddings

Crêpes Suzette

This is one of the best and most convenient puds, making the most of bitter Seville oranges in their too-short season. The finished dish freezes well: I thaw it for 3–5 hours at room temperature before putting it into the oven. **Serves 6**

4 oz/110 g butter *for the filling*
4 oz/110 g icing sugar, sieved
grated zest of 1 orange
4 tbsp brandy or orange liqueur, such as Cointreau

4 oz/110 g plain flour *for the crêpes*
2 eggs
½ pint/300 ml milk
3 tbsp melted butter or sunflower oil
grated zest of 1 orange
1 oz/25 g caster sugar
butter for frying

butter for greasing *to finish*
1–2 rounded tbsp icing sugar, sieved
3 tbsp brandy

First make the filling. Cream together the butter and the icing sugar. Beat in the orange zest, then beat in the brandy or liqueur very gradually, a teaspoonful at a time. Set aside until you have made the crêpes.

Whiz the crêpe ingredients together in a blender until well mixed, and leave for 1–2 hours. This amount of batter makes 16 crêpes.

When you are ready to start making the crêpes, drop a teaspoonful of butter into a 7-in/18-cm frying-pan. (Do not be tempted to substitute margarine: the pancakes will stick to the pan.) Melt the butter, swirling it around the pan until it is well greased. Take a large tablespoon of the pancake batter and pour it into the pan, tilting to cover the surface with a thin layer of batter. Cook over a moderate heat, until the bottom of the pancake is golden brown, then turn and cook on the other side. When the pancake is cooked on both sides, slip it on to a wire cooling rack. Repeat until the batter is used up.

Spread the orange-flavoured butter-cream evenly over the crêpes, then fold each in half and in half again, to make triangles. Butter a shallow ovenproof dish. Lay the crêpes in rows, slightly overlapping each other. If you want to freeze it, cover it with clingfilm at this point and put it into the freezer. When you are ready to cook, take it out to thaw, then finish as below.

To finish, preheat the oven to 375°F/190°C/Gas Mark 5, and put in the dish for 20 minutes, or until the buttery filling in the pancakes has melted. Take it out and dust with the icing sugar. Warm the brandy in a small saucepan and set fire to it while it is still in the pan, then pour it over the hot crêpes. Blow out the flames before they char the crêpes. Serve warm, with whipped cream.

Almond lemon tart

This is very good eaten with a dried-fruit compote.　　　　**Serves 6–8**

4 oz/110 g butter, cold from the fridge, diced *for the pastry*
5 oz/150 g plain flour
1 tbsp icing sugar
a few drops almond extract

6 oz/175 g flaked almonds, dry-fried to toast them *for the*
4 oz/110 g caster sugar *almond and*
3 large eggs *lemon filling*
5 fl oz/150 ml double cream
a few drops almond extract
juice and finely grated zest of 2 lemons

Put the pastry ingredients into a food-processor and whiz until the consistency is that of fine breadcrumbs. Pat firmly around the sides and base of a flan dish measuring about 9 in/23 cm in diameter. Put it into the fridge for at least 1 hour. Preheat the oven to 350°F/180°C/Gas Mark 4 and bake the pastry case for 15–20 minutes, until the pastry is pale golden. Take it out, and leave the oven on.

To make the filling, put the cooled toasted almonds into the food-processor with the sugar and whiz. Add the eggs one by one, then the cream, the almond extract, the grated lemon zest and, lastly, the lemon juice. Pour this into the baked pastry shell, and smooth the top. Put it into the oven and bake until the filling is set, about 15 minutes. Take it out, and serve warm, with *crème fraîche*, or whipped cream.

Apple frangipane tart

with lemon pastry

This delicious tart makes the most of the last of our excellent eating apples. Recently I met an organic-apple grower in Somerset: one of his apple varieties started fruiting in August but others were ready for picking in April the following year! British apples are far better than those produced by any other country, and many of our eating varieties are centuries old. Whatever apple you use for this recipe, never buy the dreary Golden Delicious. They are anything but. You can make and bake the pastry case several days in advance, but you must then wrap it and keep it airtight in the fridge. If you want to prepare the apples ahead you can: leave them in a bowl of water containing lemon juice, to prevent them discolouring, for 2–3 hours. Pat them dry with kitchen paper or a teatowel before you use them.

Serves 6

for the pastry
4 oz/110 g butter, straight from the fridge, diced
4 oz/110 g flour
1 oz/25 g icing sugar
a few drops vanilla extract or essence
finely grated zest of 1 lemon

for the filling
4–6 eating apples, depending on size, Cox's or similar quality
4 oz/110 g butter, softened, unsalted if possible
4 oz/110 g caster sugar
a few drops almond extract
finely grated zest of 1 lemon
1 large egg and 1 yolk, beaten together
4 oz/110 g ground almonds, dry-fried to toast
2 oz/50 g butter, melted
1 tbsp granulated sugar

Put the pastry ingredients into a food-processor and whiz until the mixture resembles fine crumbs. Press it firmly round the sides and base of a loose-bottomed flan tin about 8 in/20 cm in diameter, then leave it in the fridge for at least 1 hour. Preheat the oven to 350°F/180°C/Gas Mark 4, and bake for 20 minutes, or until the pastry is golden brown. Should the sides slip down the edges of the dish, just press them back up with a metal spoon. Remove the tin but don't turn off the oven.

Make the filling. Peel and core the apples, then quarter them and slice each quarter into 3. Beat together the butter and caster sugar until the mixture is light and fluffy. Beat in the almond extract, the lemon zest, the egg, and the almonds. Spread this mixture over the pastry base. Arrange the apple slices on top in circles, brush them with melted butter and sprinkle over the granulated sugar. Bake for 20–25 minutes, until the apples are golden. Serve the tart warm, with vanilla ice-cream or *crème fraîche*.

Lime water ice

with mango and ginger sauce

Serves 6

This is both refreshing and convenient. The water ice has to be made ahead in order to freeze, and the sauce can be made a couple of days in advance too. If you can't get mango, try using sliced melon instead.

for the water ice

8 oz/225 g granulated sugar
1 pint/600 ml water
juice and finely grated zest of 4 limes

for the sauce

3 ripe mangoes, skinned and stoned
1 tbsp sugar
1 tbsp lime or lemon juice
6 pieces of preserved ginger, drained of their syrup, and chopped neatly

To make the ice, put the sugar and water into a saucepan over a moderate heat. Stir till the sugar has dissolved, and then let it come to the boil. Boil fast for 5 minutes. Draw the pan off the heat and add the lime juice and zest. Leave it to cool. Pour the liquid into a solid polythene container and freeze. When it is slushy, tip the contents into a food-processor and whiz, then refreeze. If you leave it too long, don't worry: chip the solid ice into the food-processor, whiz then refreeze. Repeat this 4 times – you can do it over a couple of days. You will then have a smooth, easily spoonable water ice. As you start dinner, put it into the fridge to soften a little.

Chop the mangoes: half should be in neat dice, and the rest can be as rough as it comes. Reserve the neat dice, and put the rest into a food-processor, with the sugar and the lime or lemon juice. Whiz until smooth, scrape the purée into a bowl, and fold in the neatly chopped mango and the ginger. To serve, put a spoonful of water ice into each bowl, and pour over some of the sauce.

spring puddings

Espresso cream pots

These are so good to eat but also extremely convenient because they have to be made several hours in advance or the day before you want to eat them. The grated dark chocolate garnish is optional, but if you decide to use it, hold the chocolate wrapped in a double thickness of foil as you shave or grate it to prevent it melting. You might use a dark chocolate-coated coffee bean or two as an alternative, but be sure they aren't stale – they often are.

Serves 6

3 oz/75 g darkest roast (Continental) coffee beans
1¼ pints/750 ml single cream
6 large egg yolks
3 oz/75 g soft light brown sugar
4 oz/110 g best dark chocolate, coarsely grated or shaved with a potato peeler

Put the coffee beans into a heavy saucepan and crush them with a rolling-pin. Pour in the cream, and heat gently – don't let it come near boiling – for 5 minutes. Take the pan off the heat, and leave the cream to infuse with the coffee flavour for a couple of hours.

Preheat the oven to 325°F/160°C/Gas Mark 3.

Strain the cream and discard the coffee. Gently reheat the cream, while you beat together the egg yolks and sugar. Pour the hot cream into the egg mixture, a little at a time, mixing well with each addition. Pour the mixture into a jug, and then into 6 ramekins. Put the ramekins carefully into a roasting tin with enough water in it to come half-way up the sides of the ramekins. Cover them with baking parchment, and put them into the oven. Bake until the cream barely wobbles in the centre of the ramekins, about 35–45 minutes. Carefully lift the baking tray of ramekins and water out of the oven, and let the creams cool in the tin with the water.

To serve, scatter the grated or shaved dark chocolate over each ramekin.

Iced coffee cream cake

with warm dark chocolate sauce

Serves 8–10 *This is especially good served with a warm dark chocolate or caramel sauce. Truly a party pud.*

for the cake

4 oz/110g dark chocolate

2 tsp coffee essence, either Camp coffee, instant coffee liquid, or
   1 tsp coffee granules dissolved in 1 tbsp boiling water

4 large eggs

4 oz/110 g caster sugar

for the
coffee cream

½ pint/300 ml single cream

3 tsp best instant coffee granules

4 egg yolks

2 oz/50 g caster sugar

a few drops vanilla extract

a pinch ground cinnamon

2 large egg whites

2 oz/50 g icing sugar, sieved

½ pint/300 ml double cream, whipped

2–3 tbsp coffee liqueur, such as Tia Maria

grated dark chocolate, or cocoa powder, for dusting (optional)

Warm Dark Chocolate Sauce (page 56)

First make the cake. Line a 9-in/23-cm springform cake tin with a disc of baking parchment. If the tin isn't non-stick, rub the sides well with butter and dust it out with flour.

Preheat the oven to 350°F/180°C/Gas Mark 4.

Melt the chocolate with the coffee essence in a Pyrex bowl set over a saucepan of simmering water. Whisk the eggs, then gradually add the sugar and continue to whisk until the mixture is so thick and mousse-like that when you hold up the whisk it leaves a trail on the surface. Then fold in the melted chocolate quickly and thoroughly. It will form a crust on top but this doesn't matter. Scrape the batter into the prepared cake tin, smooth the top, and bake it for 20–25 minutes. Let the cake cool in the tin.

For the filling, heat the cream in a small saucepan with the coffee granules. Meanwhile, in a Pyrex bowl, beat together the egg yolks, caster sugar, vanilla extract and cinnamon. Beat in the hot coffee cream, then return the contents of the bowl to the saucepan and, over a very gentle heat, stir until the custard thickens. This will take several minutes. It should be the consistency of thick cream. From time to time put your hand against the side of the pan: don't let it become too hot to do this or the custard will curdle. Let it cool. Whisk the egg whites until they are stiff. Whisk in the icing sugar a spoonful at a time, until you have a stiff meringue.

Whip the double cream until it forms soft peaks, then add the Tia Maria. Fold the cooled coffee custard into the whipped cream, then fold in the meringue. Pour this on top of the cooled cake. If you like – I don't – you can sprinkle the cake with some coffee liqueur first. Freeze.

About 30 minutes before you wish to serve it, dip a knife into some very hot water and run it around the sides of the Iced Coffee Cream Cake. Release the springform sides and run the knife under the cake. Remove the paper base and put the iced cake on to a serving plate. It is easier to cut while it is still frozen. Also, if you like, cover the surface with grated dark chocolate or dust it with cocoa powder – emphatically not drinking chocolate. Serve, if it appeals to you (it does to me!), with Warm Dark Chocolate Sauce.

warm dark chocolate sauce

This is the best dark chocolate sauce recipe I have ever come across. Use Green and Black's cocoa powder if you can get hold of it – it is organic and perfectly delicious.

The sauce can be kept in a screw-topped jar in the fridge. It thickens when cold, but slackens again on reheating.

½ pint/300 ml boiling water
4 oz/110 g soft brown sugar
3 oz/75 g butter
3 tbsp cocoa powder
3 tbsp golden syrup – dip the spoon in boiling water to make measuring easier
½ tsp vanilla extract, or 1 tsp vanilla essence

Put all the sauce ingredients into a saucepan and stir until the sugar dissolves and the butter melts. Then bring the sauce to the boil, turn down the heat and simmer gently for 3–4 minutes. Serve it warm, or store it in a jar in the fridge when it has cooled.

Chocolate and toasted-nut squares

These toasted nutty rich pastry squares need no spoon and fork – unless you would rather eat them with vanilla ice cream. They keep well in an airtight container for a few days.

6 oz/175 g butter, straight from the fridge, diced *for the base*
3 oz/75 g soft brown sugar
8 oz/225 g plain flour
a few drops vanilla extract
3 oz/75 g chopped walnuts or pecans

4 oz/110 g butter, softened *for the topping*
6 oz/175 g soft brown sugar
2 large eggs
1 rounded tbsp flour
½ tsp baking powder
2 rounded tsp powdered cinnamon
4 oz/110 g dark chocolate chips – either buy them or chop your own
6 oz/175 g walnuts or pecans, chopped, dry-fried and cooled

Butter an oblong baking tray measuring about 9 in x 12 in/23 cm x 30 cm. Preheat the oven to 350°F/180°C/Gas Mark 4.

Put the base ingredients into a food-processor and whiz until the mixture resembles coarse crumbs. Press this out on the baking tray – dip your fingers into some flour if they become sticky as you do this. Put it into the oven and bake for 15 minutes. Remove from the oven but don't turn the oven off.

Meanwhile, beat together the butter and soft brown sugar until light and fluffy. Beat in the eggs, one at a time, then the flour and the baking powder. Stir in the cinnamon, chocolate chips, and chopped walnuts. Spread this mixture over the nutty pastry base, as evenly as you can, and return it to the oven for 25 minutes, or until the top feels firm. Cool in the tin, then cut into squares, and store in an airtight container.

Cold beetroot and orange soup with dill cream 62
Cold spiced cucumber soup 63
Carrot and coriander soup with *crème fraîche* 64
Grated cucumber, chilli and lemon mousse 65
Aubergine pâté with tomatoes and garlic 66
Antipasti 67
Grilled crab with asparagus 69
Garlic-buttered langoustines 70
Scallops stir-fried with spring onions, ginger and lime 71
Squid with garlic and parsley 72
Smoked venison with chicory leaves stuffed with cherries and
  horseradish *crème fraîche* 73
Asparagus and saffron risotto 74

Fillets of cod baked with roast vine tomatoes, shallots and chilli 75
Pepper-crusted salmon fillets with tomato and basil salsa 76
Baked fillets of sea bass with lime chilli relish 78
Warm chicken salad with chilli croûtes and a parsley dressing 80
Cold spicy lemon and orange chicken 82
Chicken in roast ratatouille 83
Lime, sesame, ginger and garlic pork fillet stir-fry 85
Pork fillet tonnato with tomato and caper salad 86
Pork fillets with prune and sage stuffing, and prune, cream, shallot
  and sage sauce 88
Pasta with red and yellow peppers, aubergines and basil 90
New potato salad with sugarsnaps, peas and asparagus with crispy bacon
  and thyme and lemon dressing 92
Baked aubergines with tomatoes, pesto, black olives and goat's cheese 93

Blackcurrant leaf water ice with peach and raspberry compote 95
Gooseberry and elderflower compote with lemon marzipan cake 96
Lemon curd parfaits with raspberries, strawberries or blueberries 98
Iced lemon meringue bombe 99
Carpaccio of pineapple with pineapple water ice 101
Raspberry and toasted-almond meringue 102
Raspberry tart 104
Strawberry and green peppercorn parfait 106
Baked strawberry and elderflower creams 107
Strawberry and elderflower lemon curd tart 108
Vanilla cream terrine with cinnamon cherries 110
Torta di Nonna 112

summer

Summer is different things to different people. In Scotland it may mean all four seasons in one: we can experience gales, rain, hail and even snow on high ground – or blissful balmy weeks when the unfortunates on the mains supply run short of water. Several years ago in July it was consistently hotter in Skye for a whole week than it was in Delhi. During extreme heatwaves, our guests from overseas invariably complain about our lack of air-conditioning – but that doesn't usually bother us. The sun, though, often burns unwary visitors to a crisp, because the air is pure and unpolluted, so there is nothing to filter out the harmful ultra-violet rays. As I write in the middle of June, yesterday was just such a day, with a slight breeze – enough to keep away the dreaded midges! – and on a walk up the hill behind our house Godfrey and I saw two of our five golden eagles, seven common blue butterflies, one fritillary and several skylarks. Today, however, we woke up to thick mist – we can't even see the mainland opposite.

Our food reflects the weather. Last night we served cold cucumber soup, langoustines with mayonnaise, then Skye-grown strawberries on a bed of vanilla cream with crisp vanilla pastry underneath. The summer dishes I have included here reflect all that I like to eat during these months – and there is plenty of choice for those who don't eat meat or fish. My suggested summer menus appear on page 260.

Most dishes can be prepared, to a greater or lesser extent, in advance, sometimes in their entirety. All use the wonderful fruit and vegetables that are now in season – cherries, strawberries, raspberries, peaches, blackcurrants and elderflower. There are cold soups, asparagus, and fish that come into their own in our waters during the summer, such as sea bass and squid. The recipes here make me want to cook and eat them all. I hope you will feel the same.

Cold beetroot and orange soup

with dill cream

Serves 6

I love beetroot, not just for their glorious colour but also for their flavour, and this soup is just as good cold as it is hot. If you like, you can add a teaspoon of horseradish to it as it is cooking – it is surprisingly complementary with beetroot. It makes a good light first course.

3 tbsp olive oil
2 medium-sized onions, skinned and chopped
3 raw beetroot, peeled and chopped
juice of 1 orange and pared rind of half
1½ pints/900 ml vegetable or chicken stock
sea salt
freshly ground black pepper
¼ pint/150 ml full-fat *crème fraîche* and chopped dill to garnish

In a saucepan heat the oil and add the chopped onions. Cook until they are soft and transparent, then add the chopped beetroot. Cook for 5–7 minutes, stirring from time to time.

Add the orange rind and stock, and bring to simmering point. Half cover the pan and simmer gently for 15 minutes, or until the beetroot is soft. Liquidize the soup until it is velvety smooth, taste and season with salt and pepper. Stir in the orange juice.

Serve at room temperature – not chilled from the fridge – with a spoonful of the *crème fraîche* mixed with chopped dill floating on each serving of soup.

Cold spiced cucumber soup

This is the most convenient soup I know, and it tastes delicious. It can be made several hours ahead and kept in the fridge, but let it rest at room temperature for an hour before serving. This allows the flavours within the soup to come alive. The one drawback to this soup is that it can't be heated up if the weather turns cold.

Serves 6

½ **cucumber, peeled, seeded and diced small** *for the garnish*
1 **tsp sea salt**
1 **tsp caster sugar**
zest of 2 lemons and juice of 1
1 **tbsp mixed finely chopped mint and snipped chives**

1½ **cucumbers, peeled and cut into chunks** *for the soup*
½ **pint/300 ml full fat milk**
1 **pint/600 g thick, creamy natural yoghurt**
1 **tsp sea salt**
a good grinding of black pepper
2 **tbsp chopped mint leaves, preferably apple mint**
1 **mild green chilli, seeded and chopped**

Mix together all the ingredients for the garnish and leave for several hours – overnight, if you like.

Put all the soup ingredients into a blender or processor and whiz until smooth. Put it into a large jug – easier for pouring into the soup plates or bowls – and cover it. Refrigerate for several hours. To serve, divide the soup between the soup plates, and put a spoonful of the marinated herbed cucumber in the centre of each serving.

Carrot and coriander soup

with *crème fraîche*

One of the joys of this soup is that, should the weather turn inclement, it tastes just as good heated up as it does cold. It can be made a day or two in advance, providing that it is kept in the fridge. If you serve it cold, remember to bring it to room temperature for an hour before serving it or the flavour will be numbed.

Serves 6

3 tbsp olive oil
2 onions, skinned and chopped
6 medium carrots, peeled and chopped
1½ pints/900 ml chicken or vegetable stock
sea salt
freshly ground black pepper
a grating of nutmeg
juice of ½ lemon
2 good handfuls coriander
¼ pint/150 ml full-fat *crème fraîche*

Heat the olive oil in a saucepan and add the onions. Sauté until they are soft and beginning to turn colour, then add the chopped carrots. Cook, stirring occasionally, for about 5 minutes. This gives the carrots a chance to begin to caramelize on the surface. Add the stock, season with salt, pepper and nutmeg. Bring the liquid to simmering point and cook gently, with the pan half covered by its lid, until the biggest piece of carrot is tender when tested with a fork. Allow it to cool, then liquidize with the lemon juice, coriander and *crème fraîche*.

If you like, you can garnish this soup with a teaspoonful of *crème fraîche* and some grated raw carrot, but I don't think it needs it.

Grated cucumber, chilli and lemon mousse

In this refreshing mousse, which is good either as a first course or for a light lunch, the grated cucumber contrasts well with the punch of the lemon, chives and chilli. It can be made a day in advance, but it doesn't freeze successfully. I like to set this in large ramekins and turn out the mousses before serving but you could set it in a terrine and serve it in slices. **Serves 6**

1 sachet gelatine powder *or* 4 sheets leaf gelatine
½ pint/300 ml chicken or vegetable stock
½ tsp dried chilli flakes, *or* ½ red chilli, seeded and finely chopped
zest and juice of 1 lemon
2 cucumbers, seeded and grated with the skin
2 tbsp snipped chives
½ pint/300 ml full-fat *crème fraîche*
sea salt
freshly ground black pepper
½ pint/300 ml double cream, whipped to soft peaks
1 large egg white

Sprinkle the powdered gelatine into the chicken stock with the chilli and leave it to soak until it is spongy. Then warm it through gently, shaking the pan, until the granules dissolve completely. Or soak the gelatine leaves in a little water, heat the stock and add the soaked leaves – they will melt almost immediately. Add the lemon juice and leave it to cool.

Mix the grated cucumber, lemon zest and chives with the *crème fraîche*. Stir in the cooled stock and gelatine mixture, and stir thoroughly. Season with salt and pepper. Leave it to begin to set, then fold in the whipped cream. Lastly, whisk the egg white with a pinch of salt until stiff and then, with a large metal spoon, fold it quickly and thoroughly through the mousse.

Oil the ramekins, or line a loaf tin – about 3 lb/1.35 kg in size – with clingfilm and either divide the mixture between the ramekins, or pour it into the lined loaf or terrine tin. Leave it to set.

To serve, run a knife around the inside of each ramekin and turn out on to individual plates. Serve with a small heap of mixed salad leaves and a couple of chive stalks crossed on top.

Aubergine pâté

with tomatoes and garlic

This is a most useful and delicious pâté. It can be made up to two days in advance, and served spread on croûtes or crostini to eat with drinks. Or you can serve it as a main course for a light summer lunch with an accompanying salad, or as a first course. Pitta bread goes well with it too.

Serves 6

3 aubergines
3 tomatoes, skinned, seeded and chopped, or ½ x 14 oz/400 g tin chopped tomatoes
½ red-skinned onion, skinned and chopped
1–2 garlic cloves, skinned and chopped
2 tbsp red wine vinegar
2 tbsp lemon juice
6 tbsp extra-virgin olive oil
1 tbsp chopped parsley
1 tbsp chopped basil
3 tbsp natural yoghurt
sea salt
freshly ground black pepper

Prick the aubergines all over with a fork, and cut off the prickly end. Roast them in a hot oven for about 30 minutes, turning them from time to time, until the skins blacken and they feel quite soft. Then let them cool on a wire rack with a baking tray underneath it to catch any juices that may seep out. Skin the aubergines, cut up the flesh and put it into a food-processor. Add the tomatoes, onion and garlic. Whiz. Add the vinegar and lemon juice, then whiz again. Gradually add the olive oil, and lastly whiz in the parsley and basil. Fold in the yoghurt. Taste, and season with salt and pepper. Scrape into a bowl, cover, and store in the fridge.

Antipasti

A large serving plate – called an ashet in Scotland – of antipasti *makes a colourful and delicious first course. It is convenient, too, because, depending on the contents of your* antipasti, *most of it can be bought. Your* antipasti *may contain no meat or you can include salami and* prosciutto. *You can serve as part of it a simple tomato and basil salad with buffalo mozzarella – not the processed rubber that masquerades as mozzarella.*

For my antipasti *collection I would choose the best black olives, two types of salami – Milano and Napolitano – mozzarella cut in strips, tomato and basil salad, cannellini beans dressed with the best olive oil in my larder, garlic, parsley and black pepper, and cauliflower and caper salad. If you decide to make the cannellini bean salad, you must start the preparation the day before you want to serve it.*

Serves 6

for the
cannellini beans

8 oz/225 g dried cannellini beans, soaked overnight
4–6 tbsp extra-virgin olive oil
2 cloves garlic, skinned and finely chopped
½ tsp sea salt
a good grinding of black pepper
2 tbsp finely chopped flat-leaf parsley

for the cauliflower
and caper salad

2 cauliflowers, cut into neat florets
extra-virgin olive oil
squeeze of lemon juice
1 tbsp capers, preserved in olive oil

4–5 slices each salami per person
3 buffalo mozzarellas, sliced or cut into fingers
6 vine tomatoes, sliced thinly, with basil strewn over them
8 oz/225 g best black olives

Simmer the beans gently until they are tender right through – beware a small hard core in the bean. This could take as long as 3 hours. Watch the level of the stock in the saucepan as they simmer, and top up with water when needed. Drain them, then put them into a bowl and dress them immediately with the olive oil, garlic, salt and pepper. Mix together well. When they are cold, stir in the chopped parsley.

Steam the cauliflower until it is tender, then put it into a bowl and dress it with the olive oil and lemon juice. Stir in the capers and leave it to cool.

Arrange the components of your *antipasti* as you choose on a large platter.

Grilled crab with asparagus

I love crab with asparagus – which is very good with most other types of shellfish, too – and try to buy it locally grown. The crisp breadcrumb and parsley top makes a good texture contrast, and can be prepared a day in advance.

Serves 6

1 lb/450 g asparagus, weighed after the tough ends of the stalk have been cut off
1½ lb/700 g crabmeat, equal quantities of brown and white mixed together
2 tsp Tabasco
¼ pint/150 ml double cream, whipped
sea salt
freshly ground black pepper
3 oz/75 g butter
3 oz/75 g day-old breadcrumbs
2 tbsp finely chopped parsley

Cut the asparagus into lengths of about 1 in/2.5 cm and steam them until they are tender. Cool them, then mix them carefully with the crab. Stir the Tabasco into the whipped cream, and fold this into the crab and asparagus. Season with salt and pepper. Divide this between 6 ovenproof dishes, cover, and keep in the fridge until you are ready to grill them.

Meanwhile, melt the butter in a sauté pan until it is foaming, then add the breadcrumbs and parsley. Stir-fry the contents of the pan until the crumbs are golden brown. Let them cool, then distribute them over the top of the crab and asparagus mixture. Heat the grill to red-hot, and pop the dishes under until they just bubble at the edges, 2–3 minutes. Keep a close eye on them – you don't want the crumbs to singe. If this looks likely, turn down the heat. Serve immediately.

Garlic-buttered langoustines

Serves 6

Forget lobster – give me our local sweet, succulent langoustines. They come in all sizes, and luxury for me is a plateful of them, with garlic and lemon butter to dip them into. Nothing could be simpler, or more delicious. But their potential as a sublime feast is ruined if they are overcooked.

5 large langoustines per person

for the garlic butter

12 oz/350 g butter
2 fat cloves garlic, skinned, finely chopped and crushed with 1 tsp sea salt
zest of 1 lemon
2 tbsp finely chopped parsley, flat-leaf if possible

Cook the langoustines a few at a time for barely 30 seconds by dropping them into boiling water. It will go off the boil as the langoustines go in, but don't wait for it to reboil. However, if the langoustines are very large, cook them for nearer a minute. Lift them out with a slotted spoon or tongs and let them cool flat, not mounded up or their heat will continue to cook them. To serve, pull off their heads, and cut down the centre of their undersides. That way, you and your guests can pick out the flesh with a fork – it is less messy than fingerbowls.

To make the garlic butter, melt the butter over a very low heat with the garlic, the lemon zest and the parsley.

To serve, arrange the langoustines on 6 plates, and divide the butter mixture between 6 small pots – ramekins, if nothing else – and put one on each plate.

Scallops stir-fried with spring onions,

ginger and lime

Scallops and crab are my favourite shellfish. They are filling, though, so you need to curb the instinct to be over-generous towards your guests! In this recipe they are combined with lime, ginger and sesame, which enhance rather than overwhelm their flavour. If you want to use this recipe as a main course, double all of the quantities given.

Serves 6

18 king (large) scallops, with the coral
3 tbsp olive oil
2 cloves garlic, skinned and very finely chopped
12 spring onions, trimmed and sliced lengthways
about 1 in/2.5 cm fresh ginger, peeled and finely chopped
1 tbsp sesame oil
2 tbsp soy sauce
zest and juice of 2 limes

With scissors, cut off the ridge of white muscle at the side of each scallop. Heat the olive oil in a large sauté pan. Put in the garlic, spring onions and ginger and cook for 2–3 minutes over a moderate heat. Raise the heat a little and add the scallops to the pan, turning after 30 seconds or so. When they are opaque they are ready. Add the sesame oil and the soy sauce to the pan, with the lime zest and juice. Let it all cook together for 1 minute, no more. Either serve the scallops whole, with the pan juices around them, or slice each scallop diagonally into 3. A mixed-leaf and herb salad makes a good accompaniment. This dish is lovely served cold, if the weather is hot.

Squid with garlic and parsley

Squid, like sea bass, prefer warmer waters so our supplies are only plentiful in the middle to late summer. They are nicest when they are simply cooked, as in this recipe. It is imperative to remove the skin completely – any thin membrane left on will be tough. Squid is no different from other shellfish in that it is ruined by overcooking, becoming rubbery if sautéed for too long.

Serves 6

2 lb/900 g squid, weighed when trimmed
6 tbsp extra-virgin olive oil
2 cloves garlic, skinned and finely chopped
½ tsp sea salt
a good grinding of black pepper
1 red chilli, seeded and finely chopped, optional
2 tbsp chopped parsley, flat-leaf if possible

Prepare the squid by gently pulling the plastic-like end of the quill that sticks out from the base of the body. The entrails should come out with it. You could ask your fishmonger to do this. Wash out the inside of the squid under running cold water. Peel off the mottled skin and inner membrane. Slice the body into rings, each about ¼-in/0.5-cm thick. Cut the tentacles into lengths of about ¾ in/1.5 cm. You can do this several hours before cooking, but cover the bowl of squid and keep it in the fridge.

To cook, heat the olive oil in a large sauté pan and add the squid and the garlic. Over a fairly high heat, stir everything around in the pan until the squid is opaque. Season with salt and pepper, and add the chilli if you are using it. Stir in the parsley just before serving. The squid can be served warm or cold, but if cold, it benefits from a further trickle of olive oil and a squeeze of lemon.

Smoked venison with chicory leaves

stuffed with cherries and horseradish crème fraîche

This is a simple first course that converts in larger quantities to a good main course. The filling for the chicory leaves can be made a day in advance.

The smoked venison I like best comes from the Tombuie Smokehouse or the Loch Rannoch Smokery – I can never make up my mind which I prefer.

If you can't get fresh cherries, or if you can't be bothered to stone them, substitute grapes, cut in half and seeded.

Serves 6

18 slices smoked venison

4 tsp horseradish sauce
½ pint/300 ml full-fat *crème fraîche*
1 lb/450 g cherries, stoned
2 tbsp snipped chives
3 heads chicory

for the stuffed chicory leaves

Mix the horseradish into the *crème fraîche* – there is no need for more seasoning – then stir in the stoned cherries and the chives.

To assemble, lay the smoked venison on each serving plate with 2 chicory leaves. Divide the cherry mixture between the leaves. Try not to assemble it much more than half an hour before eating, but if you have to, loosely cover each plate with clingfilm.

Asparagus and saffron risotto

Serves 6

*Risotto can be simple, flavoured only with garlic and rich chicken stock –
humble but immensely satisfying – or, as in this recipe, elegant. Here on
Skye I try to use Scottish-grown asparagus. All food tastes better, and is
better for us, when it is grown close to where we live.*

4 tbsp extra-virgin olive oil
3 banana shallots or 6 smaller shallots, skinned and finely chopped
12 oz/350 g risotto rice, Arborio or Carnaroli
¼ pint/150 ml dry white wine
2 pints/1.2 litres chicken or vegetable stock
½ tsp saffron strands
1 lb/450 g asparagus, trimmed and cut into 1-in/2.5-cm lengths
sea salt
lots of freshly ground black pepper
2 oz/50 g butter, cut in pieces

Heat the oil in a sauté pan, add the shallots and, over a moderate
heat, cook gently until they are soft and transparent. Add the rice,
and stir well so that each grain is coated with olive oil. This will take
2–3 minutes. Then stir in the white wine. Let it bubble gently until it
reduces away. Now pour in some of the stock, add the saffron, and
the asparagus. Mix gently, to avoid breaking the asparagus as it
cooks, and add more stock in small amounts as it is absorbed by the
rice, stirring fairly constantly. Season with salt and pepper. Add the
pieces of butter with the last of the stock – it will give a gloss to the
risotto. Serve it immediately, while it is still slightly sloppy.

Fillets of cod baked with roast vine tomatoes,

shallots and chilli

This is delicious and convenient. The tomato and shallot mixture can be roasted in advance of cooking the fish – you can even do this the previous day if it is going to make your life easier. The best cooking implement is a large, heavy-based, ovenproof sauté pan with a good, tight-fitting lid. Ask your fishmonger for thick pieces of filleted cod.

Serves 6

5 tbsp extra-virgin olive oil
1 lb/450 g shallots, preferably banana shallots, skinned
2 lb/900 g vine tomatoes
1 red chilli, seeded and sliced, or ½ tsp dried chilli flakes
1–2 fat cloves garlic, skinned and finely chopped, optional
2 tsp sea salt
6 x 6 oz/170 g pieces cod fillet, skinned
freshly ground black pepper

Preheat the oven to 400°F/200°C/Gas Mark 6.

Heat the olive oil in a large sauté pan and put in the shallots – either whole or, if they are large, cut in half. Turn them in the oil so that they are coated in it. Then put the pan into the oven for 15 minutes. Meanwhile, quarter the tomatoes. When the shallots have roasted for 15 minutes, take them out of the oven and mix with them the tomatoes, the chilli and the garlic, taking care that the tomatoes are well oiled. Then scatter over the salt and replace the pan in the oven for another 30 minutes. Turn the mixture 3 times. At the end the tomatoes should have collapsed.

If you have roasted the shallots and tomatoes in advance, reheat them before you add the cod. Push the pieces down into the vegetables, pressing them all in – they will fit. Season with pepper, put on the lid and, over a moderate heat, let the fish steam amongst the tomatoes and shallots. This will take 10–15 minutes, depending on the thickness of the fish.

This dish is good served with small pieces of potato roasted with olive oil, paprika and rosemary – their crispy texture contrasts nicely with the softness of the fish and tomatoes. Otherwise all that is needed is a green salad.

Pepper-crusted salmon fillets

with tomato and basil salsa

The inspiration for this came one night when we were eating in Skippers restaurant in Leith. I would never have thought of putting brown sugar in a crust for salmon, but it was so good, and went perfectly with a tomato and basil salad. Unlike theirs, my version includes peppercorns, and I have turned the salad into a salsa, which benefits from being made several hours in advance. You can also prepare the salmon well ahead of time.

Serves 6

for the salsa
6 vine tomatoes, skinned, seeded and diced small
1 tsp very finely chopped red onion
1 tbsp torn basil leaves
zest of 1 lime or lemon
2 sticks celery, trimmed and sliced transparently thin
2 tsp balsamic vinegar
4 tbsp extra-virgin olive oil
½ tsp sea salt

for the crust
**2 tbsp mixed 4-colour peppercorns, either coarsely ground or crushed
   in a pestle and mortar**
1 tsp sea salt, crushed
2 tbsp Demerara sugar
2 tbsp chopped parsley, preferably flat-leaf

6 x 6 oz/175 g pieces salmon fillet
2 tbsp extra-virgin olive oil

First, make the salsa – several hours ahead if possible, to give time for the flavours to develop. Carefully, so you don't squish them, mix together all the salsa ingredients, put it into a bowl, cover it with clingfilm and leave it in the fridge.

Mix together the crust ingredients. Put the salmon fillets on a baking tray lined with baking parchment, and divide the mixture between them. Press it over the surface of the fish. You can do this several hours in advance: cover the fish loosely and leave it in the fridge.

summer main courses

To cook the fish, heat the oil in a large sauté pan until it is very hot. Put the fillets into the pan, crust side downwards, and cook for 2–3 minutes, then turn them and cook for a further 2 minutes on the other side. The spitting will be horrendous, but the taste is worth it! Don't worry – some of the crust invariably falls off, but most remains sealed on to the fish.

Serve the salmon as soon as it has cooked, with a spoonful of the salsa beside it.

Baked fillets of sea bass

with lime chilli relish

I love sea bass, even though it seems to be today's fashion fish. It cooks in minutes, and the accompanying relish can be made in advance and warmed before serving. I would choose a salad of green leaves and herbs to accompany this.

Serves 6

for the lime chilli relish

4 tbsp extra-virgin olive oil

2 red onions, skinned and very finely chopped

about 2 in/5 cm ginger, peeled and grated or finely chopped

2 cloves garlic, skinned and finely chopped

2 red peppers, halved, seeded and diced small

1 green chilli, seeded and finely chopped

3 tsp sesame oil

½ tsp sea salt

2 oz/50 g sesame seeds

zest and juice of 3 limes

12 x 6–7 oz/175–200 g fillets sea bass, skinned

2 tbsp chopped parsley

sea salt

freshly ground black pepper

First make the relish. Heat the olive oil in a sauté pan and add the onions. Cook for 3–4 minutes, stirring occasionally, then add the ginger, the garlic and the peppers. Continue to cook, stirring occasionally, until the peppers are soft, up to 10 minutes. Stir in the chilli.

Meanwhile, as this is cooking, heat the sesame oil in a small saucepan then add the salt and the sesame seeds. Cook them over a moderate heat until they turn biscuit-coloured. Then stir them into the peppers with the lime zest and juice.

Preheat the oven to 350°F/180°C/Gas Mark 4.

To cook the fish, put a sheet of baking parchment on a baking tray and strew over it the parsley. Lay the fish on top, season it with salt and pepper, and cover it with another sheet of baking parchment, tucking the edges in so that the fish is enclosed. Bake for 15–20 minutes. Test after 15 minutes to see if the fish is cooked by pushing a fork into the thickest fillet. If it isn't ready, rewrap it and put it back into the oven for another 5 minutes. To serve, lift off the fish with a fish slice, leaving behind the parsley, and put it on to warmed plates. Serve with a spoonful of relish on top.

Warm chicken salad

with chilli croûtes and a parsley dressing

This is a colourful main-course salad that has everything on one plate. Use sugarsnap peas instead of green beans, if you prefer. The chilli croûtes can be flavoured with garlic instead of chilli, and can be made a day or two in advance: reheat them before serving. Parsley is an undervalued herb, and the flat-leaf variety has much more flavour than the curly sort. As for the chicken, it always pays to buy the best, which invariably means organically raised. The taste and texture of an organic chicken far surpasses that of a mass-produced specimen.

Serves 6

3 red and 3 yellow peppers, halved and seeded
6 organic chicken breasts, with skin
2 red onions, skinned and thinly sliced
3 fat cloves garlic, skinned and halved
6 tbsp olive oil
1 tsp sea salt
8 oz/225 g green beans, trimmed and sliced into lengths of about 2 in/5 cm
assorted salad leaves

for the dressing

6 tbsp extra-virgin olive oil
½ tsp sea salt
a good grinding of black pepper
½ tsp caster sugar
2 tsp Dijon mustard
2 tbsp lemon juice
2 heaped tbsp chopped flat-leaf parsley

for the croûtes

3 oz/75 g butter
1 red chilli, seeded and finely chopped
½ tsp salt
12 circles cut from a good white loaf, about 2 in/5 cm in diameter
    and ½ in/1 cm thick

Preheat the oven to 400°F/200°C/Gas Mark 6.

Lay the pepper halves skin side uppermost on a baking tray and grill until the skin forms black blisters. Put them into a polythene bag; after 10 minutes the skin should peel off easily. Slice into thick strips.

To make the croûtes, melt the butter and cook the chilli in it for 2 minutes. Season with the salt. Brush each bread disc on either side with the chilli butter, and lay them on a baking sheet lined with baking parchment. Bake in the hot oven or under the grill until they are golden and crisp. (You can do them ahead, in which case you will need only to warm them for 10 minutes at 350°F/180°C/Gas Mark 4.)

Line a roasting tin with baking parchment and put in the chicken breasts, skin side up, with the red onions and the garlic, and cover both with olive oil, mixing it into the sliced onions so that they are coated well with oil. Scatter over the sea salt. Bake for 35 minutes, stirring the onions around once or twice. Half-way through the cooking time add the sliced peppers to the tin. Test to see if the chicken is cooked through by sticking a sharp knife into the thickest part of one of the breasts. The juices should run clear. If they are tinged with pink, put them back to cook for a few minutes longer.

Meanwhile, combine all the ingredients for the dressing except the parsley; add it when you are ready to dress the salad so that it retains its colour. Steam the sliced beans until they are soft, but retaining a slight bite.

As soon as the chicken is cooked, spoon the parsley dressing over each breast. Stir the warm beans into the onions and peppers.

To assemble the salad, arrange a mixture of salad leaves on a large serving plate, and put the warm chicken breasts on top. Spoon around them the red onions, peppers and beans. Tuck the croûtes around the edges of the salad leaves, and serve.

Cold spicy lemon and orange chicken

Serves 4

This dish looks so attractive when it is ready to serve that there's no need to worry about any garnish. It's all in the ingredients!

5 fl oz/150 ml natural yoghurt

1½ tbsp orange juice

1½ tbsp lemon juice

about 1 in/2.5 cm fresh ginger, peeled and chopped

1 tsp dried chilli flakes

1 tsp coriander seeds, pulverized in a mortar with a pestle

½ tsp ground turmeric

sea salt

7 fl oz/200 ml full-fat *crème fraîche*

about 2 tbsp oil, either sunflower or olive

1 bay leaf

2 tsp 4-colour mixed peppercorns, crushed

3 cardamom pods, crushed

1–1½ lb/450–700 g chicken breast meat, cut into 1-in/2.5-cm cubes

1 tbsp chopped coriander leaves

about 12 cherry tomatoes, halved

In a mixing bowl stir together the yoghurt, orange and lemon juice, the ginger, dried chillies, coriander, turmeric, salt and *crème fraîche*.

In a sauté pan heat the oil with the bay leaf, the peppercorns and the cardamom, and cook together over a moderate heat for a couple of minutes. Then pour in the yoghurt and *crème fraîche* mixture and cook for a further minute. Add the cut-up chicken and cook, stirring from time to time, for 5–8 minutes. Stir in the chopped coriander leaves and the halved tomatoes, then cook for a further few minutes until the tomatoes have heated through. Leave it to cool. Serve cold with boiled Basmati rice or bread.

Chicken in roast ratatouille

Too many people think that making ratatouille is just a matter of chucking sautéd onions, courgettes, tomatoes and aubergines into a pot and letting them stew. If you do that, the result will be revolting: the sautéing takes ages and the vegetables, especially the aubergines, soak up a vast amount of oil as they cook. I roast my vegetables and I don't include courgettes. That way, I use a fraction of the olive oil that is needed when the vegetables are sautéd.

This ratatouille mixture freezes excellently, either alone or with the chicken. I made it for 40 people last summer and the joy of thawing and reheating such a good dish is immeasurable.

Serves 4–6

1 x 3½ lb/1.6 kg organic chicken
2 onions, peeled and halved
2 celery sticks
1 bay leaf
a few peppercorns
2 tsp sea salt

2 red onions, skinned and finely sliced   *for the*
4 tbsp olive oil – you may need more   *ratatouille*
2 tsp sea salt
3 red peppers, seeded and sliced
2 aubergines, cut into neat 1-in/2.5-cm chunks
8 vine tomatoes, quartered
2–4 fat cloves garlic, skinned and finely chopped
plenty of freshly ground black pepper

Cook the chicken, immersing it in water in a large saucepan, with the onions, celery sticks, bay leaf, peppercorns and salt. Bring it to a simmer, and cook for 15 minutes per lb/450 g. Turn off the heat and leave it to cool in the stock, then remove the chicken, strip the meat from the bones and skin, and dice it.

To make the ratatouille, preheat the oven to 400°F/200°C/Gas Mark 4, and line a roasting tin with silicon paper – or 2 if you have them.

Mix together the sliced onions and peppers with some of the olive oil, scatter over some of the salt, and roast for 20–30 minutes, until the vegetables are soft and beginning to caramelize. Stir them around during the cooking time – the outer edges cook faster than the middle. Then do the same with the aubergine chunks: rub some olive oil into them, scatter over some of the salt and put them to roast. Don't mound them up on too small a roasting tin or they will steam rather than roast. As with the onions and peppers, stir them about, outer edges into the middle, during the cooking time. Roast the quartered tomatoes with the chopped garlic in the same way. You may be surprised by how long the tomatoes take to cook – they will need a full 20 minutes.

When all the vegetables have been roasted, mix them together and season with salt and pepper. Then stir the cooked chicken through the ratatouille and serve. Or cool the ratatouille and freeze. If you don't intend to serve it at once, add the cold chicken to the cooled ratatouille. Never add hot ratatouille to cold chicken: harmful bacteria might go forth and multiply.

To reheat, put the ratatouille and chicken together into a large pan over a moderate heat, and cook until there is a gentle general bubbling. Let it simmer very gently for 15 minutes.

Lime, sesame, ginger and garlic pork fillet stir-fry

This dish is vegetables and meat all in one. It is full of complementary flavours and contrasting textures. You can substitute chicken for the pork if you prefer. The preparation can be done in advance; putting together the prepared ingredients and cooking them takes 8–10 minutes. **Serves 6**

3 tbsp extra-virgin olive oil

3 x 8–12 oz/225–350 g pork fillets, trimmed of membrane, and cut into fingers

12 spring onions, trimmed and sliced in half lengthways

2 cloves garlic, skinned and chopped

about 2 in/5 cm ginger, peeled and finely chopped

1 oz/25 g sesame seeds

8 oz/225 g sugarsnap peas, sliced diagonally into 3

zest and juice of 3 limes

1 cucumber, peeled and cut into neat fingers about 2 in/5 cm long

2 tbsp sesame oil

4 tbsp soy sauce – Superior Soy if possible, or Kikkoman's

2 oz/50 g fresh coriander, chopped

Heat the oil in a large, deep sauté pan and, over a high heat, stir-fry the strips of pork fillet until they are brown. Scoop them out on to a warm dish. Put the spring onions, garlic and ginger into the pan with the sesame seeds and the peas. Stir over a high heat for 3–5 minutes. Then add the lime zest and juice, the cucumber, sesame oil, and soy sauce. Continue to cook for a further couple of minutes before replacing the pork fillet in the pan. Cook everything together for a further 2–3 minutes. Stir in the coriander and serve immediately with boiled Basmati rice and a mixed-leaf salad.

Pork fillet tonnato

with tomato and caper salad

This dish will remind Italophiles of Vitello Tonnato. We can't buy veal in Skye, but I think pork fillets substitute well for it, though care is needed in cooking them so that the meat doesn't become dry. The sauce goes exceptionally well with the meat, although the flavour combinations might seem odd to those unfamiliar with the original.

Serves 6

3 x 1 lb/450 g pork fillets, trimmed of any fat
chopped parsley and a few capers in olive oil, to garnish

for the vegetable stock

3–4 pints/1.7–2.2 litres water
1 stick celery
1 onion, peeled and halved
1 fennel, quartered
a few parsley stalks, crushed
1 bay leaf
a little sea salt
small handful peppercorns

for the sauce

4 oz/110 g tinned tuna, drained of its oil or brine
2 egg yolks
2 anchovy fillets
½ pint/300 ml extra-virgin olive oil
a good grinding of black pepper
2 tbsp lemon juice

Put all the ingredients for the stock into a large saucepan, bring to a simmer and let it bubble gently for 20 minutes. Then with the stock barely simmering, poach the pork fillets for 20 minutes per lb/450 g. Let them cool in the stock. When they are cold, take them out of the stock and slice them thinly.

To make the sauce, put the tuna into a food-processor with the egg yolks and the anchovy fillets. Whiz, then gradually add the olive oil, in a very thin trickle. Whiz in the pepper and, lastly, the lemon juice. Taste, and adjust the seasoning – add more pepper and lemon juice if you think it is needed.

Arrange the slices of pork on a serving plate and coat them with the Tonnato sauce. Scatter over the capers, and some chopped parsley if you like. Serve with the tomato and caper salad.

tomato and caper salad

Serves 6

8 tomatoes, skinned if you like
3 tsp capers in olive oil, drained

$\frac{1}{2}$ **small red onion, skinned and finely diced**   *for the dressing*
2 tbsp extra-virgin olive oil
2 tsp balsamic vinegar
1 tsp sea salt
$\frac{1}{2}$ **tsp caster sugar**
a good grinding of black pepper

Wash the tomatoes if you are not skinning them, and slice them as thinly as possible. Arrange in a dish and scatter the capers over them. Mix together the dressing ingredients, and spoon over the tomatoes and capers.

Pork fillets with prune and sage stuffing

and prune, cream, shallot and sage sauce

This is a lovely moist stuffing, which complements the pork beautifully. The fillets can be stuffed and brushed with butter several hours in advance, providing that they are kept in a cool place. Then all you need to do is pop them into a hot oven to roast. The pork fillets are also very good served cold and sliced, with a sharp apple and ginger or plum chutney.

Serves 6

3 pork fillets weighing approx. 2½ lb/1.2 kg
2 oz/50 g butter, melted – for brushing the fillets when stuffed

for the stuffing

4 tbsp extra-virgin olive oil
1 onion, skinned and very finely chopped
3 sticks celery, strings removed and thinly sliced
3 oz/75 g fresh white breadcrumbs
6 dried prunes, chopped from their stones
4–6 fresh sage leaves, chopped
pinch of salt
plenty of freshly ground black pepper

for the sauce

2 oz/50 g butter
2 banana shallots or 3 smaller ones, skinned and very finely chopped
6 sage leaves, variegated if possible, chopped
6 no-soak prunes, stoned and chopped small
½ pint/300 ml double cream
freshly ground black pepper
½ tsp sea salt

Preheat the oven to 400°F/200°C/Gas Mark 6.

Prepare the fillets by laying them, one at a time, on a board and cutting down each lengthways with a sharp knife – don't cut right through the meat. Spread them out and cover them with clingfilm or baking parchment, then bash with a rolling-pin. Don't flatten the meat, just widen it enough to lay the stuffing along the centre.

To make the stuffing, heat the olive oil in a saucepan and sauté the onion and sliced celery until they are soft. Stir them into the bread-crumbs. Add the chopped prunes, the sage, salt and pepper and mix everything together well – I find it best to do this by hand. Divide the stuffing between each fillet and roll the meat over it. Lay the fillets on an oiled baking tray or roasting tin. Brush them generously with melted butter. Roast for 25–30 minutes, brushing with melted butter once more during the cooking time.

To make the sauce, melt the butter in a saucepan and sauté the shallots until they are soft. Add the chopped sage and prunes, then stir in the cream. Season with pepper and salt, then let the sauce bubble gently for 2–3 minutes.

To serve, slice the fillets, divide them between the plates and pour over the sauce. If you have decided not to make the sauce, serve with creamy mashed potatoes. If you have made the sauce, this dish goes well with new potatoes roasted in their skins with olive oil and rosemary, and steamed sugarsnap peas.

Pasta with red and yellow peppers,

aubergines and basil

This is delicious. It is also very convenient because the sauce can be prepared in advance and reheated as the pasta cooks. You must use full-fat crème fraîche: the reduced-fat alternative will be thin and watery around the vegetables, and the flavour too acidic. I don't serve grated Parmesan with this, but there is no reason why you shouldn't.

Serves 6

for the sauce
3 red and 3 yellow peppers
4 red onions, skinned and finely sliced
4 aubergines, cut into 1-in/2.5-cm chunks
5 tbsp extra-virgin olive oil
2 tsp sea salt
2 cloves garlic, skinned and finely chopped
2 red chillis, seeded and chopped, optional
½ pint/300 ml full-fat *crème fraîche*
a good grinding of black pepper
2 tbsp torn basil leaves

12–16 oz/350–450 g short pasta, such as penne
1 tbsp extra-virgin olive oil

Preheat the oven to 350°F/180°C/Gas Mark 4.

Halve the peppers, discard the seeds, then grill them with the skin uppermost until it blisters and turns black. Then put them into a plastic bag for 10 minutes, after which the skins should slip off easily. Chop the flesh.

Line a large roasting tin with baking parchment. Put in the sliced onions and diced aubergines then pour over the olive oil – you may need another spoonful or two. Stir it in well, so that each piece of vegetable is covered. Scatter over the salt, and roast for 35–40 minutes, moving the vegetables around the roasting tin twice during the cooking time. Then add the garlic, chillis, if you are using them, and the chopped red and yellow peppers, mixing them well with the onions and aubergines. Roast for a further 10–15 minutes.

Scoop the contents of the roasting tin into a sauté pan or saucepan. Stir in the *crème fraîche*, taste, and add more salt if you think it is needed, and the pepper. Stir in the basil just before serving: if it sits for too long in a hot sauce, it loses its flavour.

Boil the pasta in plenty of salted water until it is just *al dente*. Drain it, and mix in the olive oil to prevent it sticking together.

Serve with the sauce spooned over the pasta.

New potato salad with sugarsnaps, peas and asparagus

with crispy bacon, and thyme and lemon dressing

This salad – which, if you leave out the crispy bacon garnish, is a tasty main course for vegetarians – makes the most of the delicious new potatoes we have in the early part of the summer. It is hard to beat Jersey Royals, but Pink Fir Apple or Ratte are very good, too. If you prefer, you can leave the sugarsnaps unsteamed, in which case slice them smaller.

Depending on the assortment of salad leaves and edible petals used, this can look like the very essence of summer.

Serves 6

for the dressing

6 tbsp extra-virgin olive oil
2 tbsp lemon juice
grated zest of 1 lemon
1 tsp caster sugar
½ tsp sea salt
freshly ground black pepper
1 tsp Dijon mustard
about 3-in/7-cm sprig thyme, leaves stripped from the stems

for the salad

2 lb/900 g new potatoes, scrubbed
1 lb/450 g asparagus, tough ends removed and cut into 1½-in/4-cm lengths
1 lb/450 g sugarsnap peas, cut in 2 or 3 pieces
1 lb/450 g garden peas, weighed after shelling
assorted salad leaves and edible petals
6 rashers best streaky bacon, crisp grilled, then broken up

Put all the dressing ingredients into a jar with a good screw top and shake it vigorously to mix well.

Steam or boil the new potatoes until they are tender.

Steam the asparagus for 3 minutes, then add the sugarsnaps and peas, and continue to steam until the asparagus is tender. Tip them into a bowl, and stir in the dressing.

Cut in half any large potatoes, so that they are all more or less the same size. Mix them with the peas, asparagus and sugarsnaps, so that they all cool together and absorb the flavours from the dressing. Put the salad leaves and petals on to a large serving plate, and pile the potato salad on top. Scatter over the crispy bacon.

Baked aubergines

with tomatoes, pesto, black olives and goat's cheese

All the savoury tastes I love are here in this one dish. It is convenient and adaptable, because you can make the whole thing in advance, and reheat it before serving. Serve with chunks of bread, and a mixed-leaf and herb salad. **Serves 6**

3 fairly large or 4 smaller aubergines, thinly sliced
3 tbsp extra-virgin olive oil, plus extra for brushing the aubergine slices
3 red onions, skinned and finely diced
2 cloves garlic, skinned and finely chopped
1 pint/600 ml tomato sauce (see page 94)
about 2 dozen best black olives, stoned and halved
sea salt
freshly ground black pepper
2 tbsp pesto
6 vine tomatoes, skinned, seeded and thickly sliced
about 1 lb/450 g chèvre, or any other melting cheese, cut into ½-in/1-cm slices

Brush both sides of the aubergine slices with olive oil, and put them on to a foil-lined baking tray. Either grill them on both sides until they are brown or roast them on a parchment-lined tray in a hot oven, 400°F/200°C/Gas Mark 6, for 20 minutes. Turn down the oven to 350°F/180°C/Gas Mark 4 if you plan to eat the finished dish straight away.

Meanwhile, heat the 3 tablespoons of olive oil in a sauté pan and sauté the red onions and garlic until they are soft and beginning to caramelize.

Rub an ovenproof dish about 8 x 10 in/20 x 25 cm with olive oil. Spoon the tomato sauce over the bottom of the dish, and dot the olives over it. Arrange the aubergine slices over the olives, season with salt and pepper, and spread them with pesto. Lay the tomato slices on top and, if the dish will take them, repeat the layers of aubergines and tomatoes. Cover the surface with the cheese. Put the dish under a fairly hot – but not red-hot – grill, until the surface of the cheese melts. Then put the dish into the oven for 10 minutes. Serve warm. If you are going to prepare the dish in advance and reheat it when you need it, you will not need to grill the cheese to melt it. Simply heat the dish in a moderate oven, 350°F/180°C/Gas Mark 4, until the sauce is bubbling – around 20–25 minutes.

tomato sauce

This sauce is amazingly versatile – delicious with vegetables, fish or on pizzas – and has the added bonus of being low in calories. If you are making it in summer, when fresh basil is available, add the basil when you purée the sauce. I think that fresh basil loses its pungency in cooking.

Makes about 1½ pints/900 ml

5 tbsp olive oil
2 onions, skinned and chopped
1 celery stalk, cut into 1-in/2.5-cm chunks, optional
1 red pepper, halved, seeded and chopped
2 x 14 oz/400 g cans tomatoes *or* 1½ lb/675 g fresh tomatoes,
　skinned, halved and seeded
½ tsp sugar
1 large garlic clove, skinned and chopped
sea salt
freshly ground black pepper
1 tbsp torn fresh basil leaves, *or* 1 tsp dried basil

Heat the oil in a saucepan and sauté the onions for 5 minutes, stirring occasionally. Add the celery and red pepper, and cook for a further 2–3 minutes. Put in the tomatoes, sugar, garlic, seasoning and dried basil, if you are using it. Let the sauce simmer, uncovered, for 25–30 minutes. Allow to cool slightly, then pour into a blender or food-processor. Add the fresh basil, if you are using it, and blend until smooth.

This sauce freezes well, and keeps in the fridge for 2–3 days.

Blackcurrant leaf water ice

with peach and raspberry compote

*This simple but convenient pudding makes the most of our seasonal fruits –
and their leaves. I always include a good bunch of blackcurrant leaves in a
saucepan of blackcurrant jam: the blackcurrants mask the taste of the leaves,
but they add a haunting depth to the flavour of the finished product. The
water ice is superbly complemented by the raspberries and peaches.
Blackcurrant leaves give the taste of muscat grapes.*

Serves 6

1½ pints/900 ml cold water *for the*
10 oz/275 g granulated sugar *water ice*
pared rind and juice of 2 lemons
2 large handfuls blackcurrant leaves

6 peaches *for the*
2 lb/900 g raspberries *compote*
3 tbsp caster sugar

Put the cold water and the sugar into a saucepan with the lemon
rind. Stir over a moderate heat until the sugar has dissolved, then boil
the syrup fast for 5 minutes. Take the pan off the heat, add the
lemon juice and the blackcurrant leaves, then leave it to stand until it
is cold. Strain the liquid, discarding the leaves and the lemon rind,
and pour it into a solid polythene container. Freeze. When it has
almost set, take the container from the freezer and chip the contents
into a food-processor. Whiz, and refreeze. Repeat 4 times. The water
ice will be almost spoonable from the freezer but, to be sure, put the
container into the fridge for 30 minutes before you want to eat the
ice.

Pour boiling water over the peaches in a bowl. Leave them for 30
seconds then drain off the water. The skins should peel off easily.
Cut each in half, twist the halves in opposite directions, and flick out
the stones. Slice each peach half into 6 and put the slices into a
serving bowl. Carefully – so as not to break up the peach slices – fold
the raspberries and sugar among them. Serve with the blackcurrant
leaf water ice.

Gooseberry and elderflower compote

with lemon marzipan cake

Serves 6

I do believe that the world is divided into those who love gooseberries and those who can't bear them. Sadly, Godfrey and I are like Jack Spratt and his wife about gooseberries: I love them, but he would rather starve than eat one. In this recipe, the exquisite flavour of elderflower enhances that of the gooseberries. If you prefer, you can use honey instead of the sugar to sweeten the compote.

2 lb/900 g gooseberries, topped and tailed
2 good handfuls elderflower heads
6 oz/175 g granulated sugar
½ pint/300 ml water

Put the gooseberries, elderflower heads, sugar and water into a saucepan, preferably not aluminium, with a lid on the pan. Cook over a moderate heat until the gooseberries have collapsed, and are soft. Let them cool, then fish out the elderflowers and throw them away. Pour the compote into a serving bowl.

lemon marzipan cake

Serves 6

This cake keeps well and has a lovely gungy texture.

6 oz/175 g butter
6 oz/175 g caster sugar
3 large eggs
6 oz/175 g ground almonds, dry-fried to toast them
zest of 2 lemons
a few drops almond extract

for the icing (optional)

juice of ½ lemon, or more
3 oz/75 g icing sugar, sieved

Preheat the oven to 300°F/150°C/Gas Mark 2. Butter an 8-in/20-cm cake tin, and line the base with a disc of baking parchment.

In a bowl, beat together the butter and sugar until the mixture is light and fluffy. Beat in the eggs, alternating with the ground almonds, until you have a smooth cake batter. Lastly, beat in the lemon zest and the almond extract. Scrape it into the prepared cake tin. Bake for 40 minutes. Then push a skewer into the middle of the cake: if it comes out covered in raw cake goo, put it back into the oven for a further 10–15 minutes, then test again. The skewer should have some stickiness even when the cake is cooked, but it shouldn't be raw. Let the cake cool in the tin, then turn it out and, if you like, make the icing.

Mix the lemon juice into the sieved icing sugar and pour the icing over the surface of the cake. Let it trickle down the sides.

Keep the cake in an airtight container until you are ready to serve it.

Lemon curd parfaits

with raspberries, strawberries or blueberries

This is one of my favourite summer puds. The sharply flavoured lemon curd – to which you can add elderflowers in season – can be made several days in advance. Lemon enhances all soft summer fruit, except gooseberries. The lemon curd can be made and kept in the fridge for 4–5 days. Assemble the parfait in the morning for serving in the evening.

Serves 6

1 lb/450 g berries – chopped strawberries, raspberries, blueberries

for the lemon curd

4 oz/110 g butter, diced

2 large egg yolks and 1 large egg, beaten together

4 oz/110 g caster or granulated sugar

zest of 3 lemons

juice of 2 lemons

for the parfaits

½ pint/300 ml double cream, whipped to soft peaks

2 large egg whites

2 oz/50 g icing sugar, sieved

a few drops vanilla extract

Put all of the lemon curd ingredients into a Pyrex bowl and set it over a saucepan of simmering water. Stir until the butter melts and the sugar dissolves. Continue to stir from time to time as the curd thickens. When it is very thick, take the bowl off the heat, and leave it to cool.

To make the parfaits, whisk the egg whites, and when they are stiff gradually whisk in the icing sugar until you have a stiff meringue. Put some berries into 6 glass serving dishes or glasses. Fold the meringue mixture into the whipped cream, with the vanilla extract, then fold in the lemon curd, leaving it streaky. Divide the parfait between the glasses. Serve, if you like, with crisp lemon, almond or shortbread biscuits.

summer puddings

Iced lemon meringue bombe

Golly, this is good. It is the sort of thing that I could find myself polishing off alone in the larder. You can make it 3–4 weeks in advance, and keep it in the freezer. On the day, take it out of the freezer and turn it on to a serving plate just before you serve dinner. It will taste much better than straight from the freezer.

Serves 6–8

3 large egg whites *for the*
a pinch of salt *meringues*
6 oz/175 g caster sugar

1 whole egg and 3 yolks (from the meringues), beaten together well *for the*
4 oz/110 g caster or granulated sugar, sieved *lemon curd*
4 oz/110 g butter, diced
zest and juice of 2 large, juicy lemons

3 large egg whites *for the*
a pinch of salt *ice cream*
3 oz/75 g sieved icing sugar
½ pint/300 ml double cream, whipped with a few drops of vanilla extract

Start by making the meringues. Preheat the oven to 225°F/110°C/ Gas Mark ¼. Whisk the egg whites with the salt until they are stiff then, whisking continuously, add the sugar a spoonful at a time. When you have a good stiff meringue, line a baking tray with a sheet of baking parchment and spoon even-sized dollops of meringue mixture on to it. Bake for 2½–3 hours, then take them out and leave them to cool.

Put the lemon curd ingredients into a Pyrex bowl, over a saucepan of simmering water. Stir until the butter has melted and the sugar dissolved. Then stir occasionally as the lemon curd thickens. Take the bowl off the heat and let it cool. When the lemon curd is cold and the meringues are cooked and cooled – you could make them at different times if that is more convenient – make the ice cream.

Whisk the egg whites with a pinch of salt. When they are stiff, whisk in the icing sugar a spoonful at a time. Now whip the cream, with the vanilla extract. Fold the meringue into the cream. Crush the cooked meringues and fold them with the cold lemon curd through the cream mixture. You will be amazed by how the crushed meringues seem to reduce in volume as you fold them in.

Line a bowl of about 4 pints/2.2 litres capacity with clingfilm, and pack the mixture into it. Place a disc of baking parchment on top, cover with clingfilm, and freeze. If you like, you can serve this with a purée of raspberries, or strawberries flavoured with elderflower syrup.

Carpaccio of pineapple with pineapple water ice

This is a perfect pud to end a summer dinner. Or, for that matter, a dinner at any time of the year. The key to its success or otherwise is that the pineapples should be juicy, not woody and dry. The pineapple water ice has to be made several days ahead, and the thin slicing for the carpaccio can be done several hours in advance. Remember to take the water ice out of the freezer and put it into the fridge before you start dinner.

Serves 6

1 pint/600 ml cold water *for the water ice*
6 oz/175 g granulated sugar
juice and pared rind of 1 lemon
1 pineapple, or 2 if they are small, peeled, cored and cut into chunks

2 ripe pineapples *for the carpaccio*
3 oz/75 g crushed pistachio nuts, dry-fried, optional

To make the water ice, put the water and sugar into a saucepan with the lemon rind. Stir over a moderate heat until the sugar has dissolved, then boil for 5 minutes. Take the pan off the heat, stir in the lemon juice and the pineapple, then leave it to cool. When it is cold, remove the lemon rind and liquidize the contents of the pan. Pour this slushy mixture into a solid polythene container and freeze it. After several hours take it out of the freezer, and whiz the mixture in a food-processor. Refreeze. Repeat 3 times – if it freezes solid, chip it into the food-processor. Each time you whiz it, you will find it becomes progressively easier to spoon out of its container.

To make the carpaccio, cut the skin from the pineapples with a serrated knife, nicking out the tiny brown indentations. With a very steady hand, slice the pineapples as thinly as you possibly can.

To assemble, put 3 wafer-thin slices of pineapple, overlapping, on each plate before you begin dinner, then cover them with a cloth or clingfilm to prevent them drying out. Put a spoonful of pineapple water ice in the middle of each plate, on top of the pineapple. Scatter over a few pistachios and serve.

Raspberry and toasted-almond meringue

This is so simple, but such an indulgence for me because I so love toasted nutty meringues. It's a useful pud too, because the meringues can be made up to a week in advance, providing they are kept in an airtight container. You can freeze them too, but put them in a tin to prevent them chipping or breaking in the freezer: although they are fragile they thaw undiminished after a couple of weeks spent thus.

Serves 6–8

4 large egg whites
a pinch of salt
8 oz/225 g caster sugar
4 oz/110 g flaked almonds, dry-fried until golden brown, then cooled

for the filling
1½ pints/900 ml double cream
1 oz/25 g caster sugar
3 tbsp Amaretto, optional
1 lb/450 g raspberries, crushed with a fork, plus a few extra for garnish
icing sugar

Preheat the oven to 225°F/110°C/Gas Mark ¼. Line two 9-in/23-cm diameter non-stick loose-bottomed cake tins each with a disc of baking parchment.

In a large bowl whisk the egg whites with the salt until they are stiff, then add the caster sugar, a spoonful at a time, whisking continuously. Then scatter in the toasted flaked almonds. Try not to fold them in – rather, incorporate them into the meringue as you divide it between the cake tins. Smooth the mixture, but don't take it right up to the edges of the tin: leave about 1 in/2.5 cm between the edge of the meringue and the rim of the tins. Bake for 2½–3 hours. Then take them out of the oven and let them cool enough for you to peel off the discs of baking parchment. It is easier to do this while the meringues are still warm.

For the filling, whip the cream with the sugar and the Amaretto, if you are using it. Fold in the crushed raspberries. Put a dab on to the serving plate and lay one meringue on it. This will anchor it and prevent it skidding off the plate. Pile the rest of the raspberry cream on to the meringue, smoothing it even. Put the other meringue on top, press it down gently, then sieve over a dusting of icing sugar, and scatter a few raspberries around it. Leave for at least 3 hours: this settles the meringue, and makes it easier to cut.

Raspberry tart

You can use any fruit, or a combination, instead of raspberries on their own. It is equally delicious with strawberries. If I use fresh apricots I poach them gently for barely 5 minutes, in a light sugar syrup, before putting them into the tart. You can make the crème pâtissière – *the vanilla custard – a day in advance, so that on the day when you want to eat the tart you need only assemble it. The pastry base can be made and baked 4–5 days in advance, in which case it will need to be stored in an airtight container or covered with clingfilm and stored in a thick polythene bag.*

Serves 6

for the pastry
4 oz/110 g butter, hard from the fridge, diced
4 oz/110 g flour
1 oz/25 g icing sugar
a few drops vanilla extract

for the crème pâtissière
¾ pint/450 ml single cream
a few drops vanilla extract *or* a split vanilla pod
5 large egg yolks
1 level tsp cornflour
3 oz/75 g caster sugar

to finish
1½ lb/700 g raspberries
8 oz/225 g redcurrant jelly, melted

Preheat the oven to 350°F/180°C/Gas Mark 4.

Put the pastry ingredients into a food-processor and whiz to the texture of fine crumbs. Press this firmly around the sides and base of an 8-in/20-cm flan dish – metal or ceramic. Put it into the fridge for at least 1 hour, then bake for 20–25 minutes, until the pastry is biscuit-coloured. Should the pastry slip down the sides of the dish during the cooking time, just push it up with the back of a metal spoon. It sometimes does this if the pastry isn't cold enough, or if the oven is a little cooler than it should be.

Now make the *crème pâtissière*. Heat the cream without boiling with the split vanilla pod or the vanilla extract. Beat together the egg yolks, cornflour and caster sugar, then beat in some of the cream. Gradually stir the rest of the cream into the egg mixture, and either cook this vanilla custard in the bowl over a saucepan containing simmering water, which will take about 35 minutes, or cook it in a microwave oven. Put the bowl on high for 1 minute, then take it out and beat the hot, creamy mixture. Put it back for 30 seconds on medium, take it out and beat the custard. Repeat until the custard is thick. If you proceed with caution, you won't curdle it. When it is cooked, take out the vanilla pod if you have used one, scraping it well to include the seeds in the custard. Let the custard cool, and when it is quite cold and very thick, spread it over the base of the baked pastry case.

Note I have recently discovered that if you use gelatine in the custard it makes slicing the tart easier and the slices neater. Simply soak two leaves of gelatine in a little cold water for 10 minutes, lift the soaked gelatine from the water and drop into the hot custard. It will dissolve immediately. Stir well and leave to cool.

Arrange the raspberries in circles over the custard. When the raspberries are used up, and the surface of the tart is covered, brush the redcurrant jelly glaze over everything – the raspberries, and the pastry edges of the tart.

Strawberry and green peppercorn parfait

This may sound a bit odd, but green peppercorns, drained of their brine and rinsed in a sieve under running cold water, combine in a syrup to form a delicious counterpart to the strawberries. You can either put the crushed strawberries into the creamy mixture, as described in the recipe, or in the bottom of a glass bowl or individual glasses, with the parfait spooned on top. Don't make this lovely pudding with the strawberries you buy in winter, which have been flown from the other side of the world: the flavour just won't be there.

Serves 6   *This should be made on the same day you want or intend to eat it.*

1 pint/600 ml cold water
6 oz/175 g granulated sugar
pared rind of 2 lemons
juice of 1 lemon
3 tsp green peppercorns, drained, rinsed (see above) and dried
2 lb/900 g strawberries, hulled
2 large egg whites
a pinch of salt
2 oz/50 g icing sugar, sieved
½ pint/300 ml double cream, whipped

Put the water, sugar and lemon rind into a saucepan over a moderate heat. Stir until the sugar has dissolved, then boil fast for 5 minutes. Take the pan off the heat and add the lemon juice and the peppercorns. Leave to cool, then pick out the strips of lemon rind. Put the strawberries into a bowl, crush them with the back of a fork and pour the cold syrup with the green peppercorns over them. Mix together well and leave to marinate for a couple of hours.

Drain off the liquid from the marinade, taking care not to lose any peppercorns. Whisk the egg whites with the salt until they are stiff, then whisk in the icing sugar, a little at a time. Fold the crushed strawberries and green peppercorns into the whipped cream, then fold in the meringue mixture with a large metal spoon. Pile the parfait into a glass or china serving bowl, or divide it between individual glasses.

summer puddings

Baked strawberry and elderflower creams

I like to serve these creams with strawberries sliced and marinated in elder-flower cordial. You can vary the fruit purée in the creams according to season – raspberries or blackberries work well. They can be made the day before, but I never freeze them.

Serves 6

1 lb/450 g strawberries, hulled
3 tbsp elderflower cordial
½ pint/300 ml single cream
2 large eggs
3 large egg yolks

Preheat the oven to 200°F/100°C/Gas Mark 1–2.

Whiz the berries in a food-processor with the elderflower cordial until you have a smooth purée, then sieve it to get rid of the tiny woody seeds.

Beat together the cream, eggs and yolks. Then stir in the straw-berry and elderflower purée. Butter 6 large ramekins. Divide the strawberry cream between them, and put them into a roasting tin with water coming half-way up their sides. Carefully put the tin into the oven for 1 hour. Then gently press the top of one of the creams: if it is very soft continue the slow cooking until it has set. Serve cold.

Strawberry and elderflower lemon curd tart

This is a perfect way to make the most of locally grown strawberries. I stress the 'local' because it is an indisputable fact that they taste so much better when they come from close to where you live. The tart has a rich, vanilla-flavoured pastry base, spread with elderflower lemon curd. You can make a jar (or more) of elderflower lemon curd up to a week before you intend to make the tart. You can bake the pastry case a couple of days in advance, providing that after baking, when it is cold, you store it in an airtight polythene bag. Assemble the tart on the morning of the day on which you intend to eat it. Lemon and elderflower accentuate the flavour of straw-berries better than anything else I know.

Serves 6

for the
elderflower
lemon curd

3 oz/75 g butter, cut into bits
4 oz/110 g sugar, either caster or granulated, it doesn't matter
2 tbsp elderflowers
1 large egg and 2 yolks, beaten well together
zest and juice of 2 lemons

for the pastry

4 oz/110 g butter, hard from the fridge, diced
4 oz/110 g plain flour
1 oz/25 g icing sugar
a few drops vanilla essence or extract

to finish

2 lb/900 g strawberries, either left whole or cut in half, depending on their size and shape
1 pot redcurrant jelly, homemade if possible, melted

Put all the curd ingredients into a Pyrex bowl, and set it over a saucepan containing gently simmering water. Stir occasionally as the butter melts and the sugar dissolves. As the curd thickens, keep stirring occasionally. Sieve the hot, thickened curd, then pot it, cover, and store it in the fridge.

Put the pastry ingredients into a food-processor and whiz until the mixture resembles fine crumbs. Flour your fingers then press the crumbs firmly around the sides and the base of an 8-in/20-cm flan dish. Put it into the fridge for at least an hour, then bake at 350°F/180°C/Gas Mark 4, until the pastry is a light biscuit-colour. If it should slip down the sides of the flan dish just push it back with a metal spoon.

To assemble the tart, spread the elderflower lemon curd over the pastry base. Arrange the strawberries in circles until the whole surface is covered. Brush the melted jelly over the entire surface – pastry edges, the lot. You can serve it with cream if you like, but I prefer it without.

Vanilla cream terrine with cinnamon cherries

This can be made in entirety the day before it is needed, or you could just cook the cherries in advance – here, you will find a cherry-stoner invaluable. If you don't have one, do invest in one – it will stone olives too. The trick with the terrine is not to use too much gelatine: the vanilla custard contains egg yolks to thicken it, but gelatine is still needed for a set that will slice easily.

Serves 6

for the cinnamon cherries

2 lb/900 g cherries, stoned
5 fl oz/150 ml fresh orange juice
3 oz/75 g caster sugar
1 cinnamon stick

for the terrine

1 fresh vanilla pod – it should be glossy and pliable
1½ pints/900 ml single cream
6 large egg yolks
3 oz/75 g caster sugar
6 sheets leaf gelatine, preferably, *or* 1½ sachets powdered gelatine

Put the stoned cherries into a saucepan with the other ingredients and, over a moderate heat, cook them gently until the cherry juices run. Leave them to cool. Try to remember to fish out the cinnamon stick.

Slit the vanilla pod lengthways and put it into a saucepan with the cream. Over a moderate heat, let the cream warm until a skin forms – don't let it come near boiling point. Take the pan off the heat, and let the cream infuse with the vanilla pod, until it is cold. Scrape the pod to include its seeds in the cream.

Beat the egg yolks well with the caster sugar. Reheat the cream gently, and mix a little with the egg mixture, then stir in the rest and return it all to the saucepan. Depending on your courage, and the quality of your saucepan, you can either cook the vanilla cream over a very gentle heat, stirring continuously, until the custard thickens to the point where it coats the back of your wooden spoon, or pour the mixture into a Pyrex bowl and cook it in a microwave oven. Give it

1 minute on high, stir it well, then give it 30 seconds on medium, stir it well, and repeat until the cream has thickened. Microwaves vary, so it is impossible to be exact as to how long this will take.

Meanwhile, soak the gelatine leaves in cold water. If you are using powdered gelatine, soak it in 4 tablespoons of cold water until it is spongy. Lift the jelly-like soaked leaves from the water and drop them into the hot thickened custard: they will dissolve almost instantly. Or stir the spongy powdered gelatine into the hot custard: it will take a little longer to dissolve. Remove the vanilla pod.

Pour the creamy custard into a Pyrex or metal terrine or loaf tin, and leave it to set. To turn it out, dip the tin or dish briefly into hot water and invert it on to a serving plate. Depending on the plate, you can spoon the cooked cherries around it, or serve them separately in a glass or china bowl.

Torta di Nonna

I discovered this light sponge cake, with its vanilla crème pâtissière, and the pine kernels on top, on a visit to Rome. When I came home I decided to make my own. The only change I have made to the original is in dry-frying the pine kernels, which I think taste even better toasted. You can serve a bowl of strawberries or raspberries with this, or indeed any of the fruity compotes in this section.

Serves 6

for the cake base
3 large eggs
6 oz/175 g caster sugar
5 oz/150 g plain flour and 1 oz/25 g cornflour, sieved together twice

for the crème pâtissière
1 pint/600 ml single cream
5 large egg yolks – keep the whites for making meringues
4 oz/110 g caster sugar
a few drops of vanilla extract
2 leaves gelatine *or* 2 level tsp powdered gelatine, soaked in 1 tbsp water

to finish
1 tbsp icing sugar, sieved
6 oz/175 g pine kernels, dry-fried until golden

Preheat the oven to 350°F/180°C/Gas Mark 4. Line a 9-in/23-cm diameter cake tin with a disc of baking parchment.

Whisk the eggs and caster sugar together until the mixture holds its shape on the surface when it trails off the whisk. Fold in the flours thoroughly, then pour the cake batter into the prepared tin. Smooth the top, and bake for 20–25 minutes. Let it cool for a minute in the tin, then carefully run a knife around the inside and turn out the cake on to a wire cooling rack. Leave it to get cold.

Meanwhile make the crème pâtissière. Heat the cream to scalding point. Beat the egg yolks and sugar with the vanilla extract, then beat in a small amount of the hot cream. Beat in the rest, then pour it into a Pyrex bowl set over a saucepan of simmering water and stir continuously until it thickens. This will take about 35 minutes.

Alternatively you could use a microwave oven: put the bowl into the oven for 1 minute on medium, take it out and beat well, then return it for another 30 seconds on medium. By now it should be very thick, but if not, give it another minute on medium. Add the gelatine and stir until it has dissolved. Leave it to get cold. Then put the cake on a serving dish and spread it thickly with the crème pâtissière.

When the crème pâtissière has set, sprinkle over the icing sugar and pine kernels.

love each season, but I become impatient for autumn. It arrives early in Skye: towards the end of August the leaves start to change colour on the large chestnut tree in the Kilmore churchyard, heralding the onset of autumn. After that, the bracken turns to gold and then russet, before it dies back. The purple heather, which starts in mid-August, might continue far into September, October and even, one memorable year, November, but just how long it lasts depends on the amount of rain we have. With rain, the purple becomes rusty before the heather dies back.

The best aspect of autumn, though, is that it is the most prolific time of year for wild-growing foods. First there are field mushrooms – some years we have few, some years none at all, and in others we can pick in the morning and again at the same places later that day. Other wild fungi are fantastic in our woods: we have chanterelles, several different species of cep, and there's one secret place where horns-of-plenty grow, known only to me and to Jenny Aldridge, our neighbour and friend.

Brambles can be prolific but, as with everything else, the crop depends on the amount of rain that falls while they are fruiting. I reckon to start picking brambles in mid-September.

Rowanberries not only look spectacular but make such good jelly – lovely with venison and roast game birds. Hazelnuts are ready to pick later in the autumn. When you eat a fresh one you realize straight away how superior they are to the ready-shelled nuts we buy in shops. Nuts freeze well, so that freshness can be preserved.

When I first smell autumn – and it does have its own smell – my spirits rise and my fingers itch to get outside with a basket for brambles or rowanberries. I look forward to eating them in dishes that especially appeal when the evenings darken and the temperature lowers. I hope that you will find in the following recipes some autumn-enhancing ideas.

Wild mushroom consommé

Serves 6   *This is a light, simple first course. I like it based on a chicken stock.*

2 pints/1.2 litres chicken stock, fat skimmed off
1 lb/450 g assorted wild mushrooms – chanterelles, horns-of-plenty,
   shiitake, chopped small
sea salt
freshly ground black pepper
3 tbsp dry sherry

Bring the stock to simmering point, and add the chopped wild mushrooms. Simmer gently for 7–10 minutes. Taste, and season with salt and pepper. Stir in the sherry. Serve.

Roast butternut squash and cumin soup

Butternut squash are available all over the country now. I have even found them in an organic farm shop in a remote part of Perthshire. Some squashes can be dull, but butternut is delicious. I like to roast it, skinned and cut into chunks, before whizzing it into the rest of the soup ingredients. Cumin, like all other spices, has so much more flavour if you buy the whole seeds rather than ready-ground.

Serves 6

2 butternut squash, peeled and cut into 2-in/5-cm chunks
6 tbsp olive oil
2 tsp sea salt, plus a little extra
2 medium onions, skinned and chopped
1 clove garlic, skinned and chopped, optional
1 tsp cumin seeds
2 pints/1.2 litres chicken or vegetable stock
freshly ground black pepper
about 2 tbsp chopped flat-leaf or curly parsley

Preheat the oven to 400°F/200°C/Gas Mark 6. Line a baking tray with baking parchment. Lay the chunks of squash on it, and rub them with 4 tablespoons of the olive oil. Scatter over the salt and roast for 30 minutes, moving the outer chunks to the centre of the baking tray once or twice during that time. The roast squash should be very soft – if not, give it another 10 minutes.

Meanwhile, heat the remaining 2 tablespoons of olive oil in a saucepan and add the onions. Sauté them over a moderate heat until they are soft and transparent. Add the garlic and the cumin and cook for a few minutes. Add the stock, bring it to simmering point, and cook for 10 minutes, very gently. Then liquidize the contents of the saucepan with the roast squash, and pour the soup into a clean saucepan. Taste, and adjust the seasoning.

To serve, reheat and, at the last minute, stir the chopped parsley through the soup to perk up its appearance.

Spicy cauliflower soup

I love soup. It is both convenient and so variable in content and texture that it can satisfy on many different occasions. This is an intensely flavoured fairly thin soup, and makes a light first course. Kath Stevenson made it first at Kinloch. The chillis supply the spiciness – and chilli releases endorphins in the brain, which create euphoria. What fun to achieve this by legal and edible means rather than illicit ones!

It can be made a couple of days in advance, kept in the fridge, and reheated before serving. I use chopped flat-leaf parsley as the simple garnish – I don't want to introduce any other flavour to this particular soup.

Serves 6

4 tbsp olive oil
2 medium onions, skinned and chopped
1 medium cauliflower
2 pints/1.2 litres chicken or vegetable stock
1 level tsp dried chilli flakes
sea salt
freshly ground black pepper
a grating of fresh nutmeg
2 tbsp chopped flat-leaf parsley

Heat the oil in a saucepan and sauté the onions in the oil until they are soft and transparent, about 5–7 minutes. Meanwhile, cut off the outer leaves, trim the stem, and cut the cauliflower into small chunks. When the onions are soft, add the cauliflower to the pan, with the stock, and the chilli. Bring it to a gentle simmer, half cover the pan, and cook very gently for 15 minutes, or until the thickest bit of stalk is tender right through when you test it with a fork.

Liquidize the contents of the pan and return the soup to a clean saucepan. Taste, then season with salt, pepper and nutmeg. To serve, reheat and stir the parsley through the soup at the last minute.

Tomato, pear and horseradish soup

The sweetness of the pear is counteracted by the sharpness of the horse-radish. I like to use chicken stock, and you can opt either for fresh tomatoes or canned ones. The soup can be made a couple of days in advance, providing it is kept in the fridge. Again, it makes a light first course.

Serves 6

3 tbsp olive oil
2 onions, skinned and chopped
1 stick celery, strings removed and sliced
2 ripe pears, with skin and core, but stalks removed, chopped
1 x 14 oz/400 g tin chopped tomatoes
2 pints/1.2 litres good stock, either vegetable or chicken
1 tbsp creamy horseradish sauce
sea salt
freshly ground black pepper
a basil leaf or a few snipped chives for each serving

Heat the oil in a saucepan and sauté the onions for a few minutes. Add the sliced celery and continue to cook until the onions are soft, and starting to caramelize. Then add the chopped pears, the tomatoes, the stock and the horseradish sauce. Bring it to simmering point, and cook gently for 5–10 minutes. Take it off the heat, let it cool, then liquidize and sieve it. Taste, and season with salt and pepper. To serve, reheat and garnish simply with a basil leaf or some chives on top of each helping.

Spiced beetroot and carrot salad with garlic

We are constantly being told we should eat more raw vegetables, which sounds such a bore, but this salad is anything but: you will enjoy eating what is good for you! I like to serve it on a bed of leaves. It makes a perfect first course before a rich main course.

Serves 6   *A mandolin makes light work of the carrot and beetroot preparation.*

½ tsp mustard seeds
¼ tsp fennel seeds
½ tsp coriander seeds
3 cardamom pods, husks removed
2 fat cloves garlic, skinned
1 tbsp sea salt
5 tbsp extra-virgin olive oil
3 tbsp fresh lemon juice
2 tsp white wine vinegar
a dash of Tabasco
2 lb/900 g raw carrots, peeled and sliced into thin matchsticks,
    about 2 in/5 cm long
1 lb/450 g raw beetroot, prepared in the same way as the carrots
2 tbsp snipped chives
1 tbsp chopped parsley

Put the spices in a mortar and pound them with the pestle. Bash the garlic on a board with the salt. Mix the garlic with the pounded spices and gradually stir in the olive oil, lemon juice, vinegar and Tabasco. Put the carrots and beetroot into a mixing bowl, and stir in the dressing with the chives and parsley. Turn the salad into a serving bowl or put it on individual plates. It will benefit from being dressed several hours before it is eaten – so that the flavours can mingle and mature.

Tomato and red onion salad

with green dressing

Cheese sablés (page 124) go well with this salad. Late-season tomatoes give us a last-minute taste of summer before we have to buy imported ones. Allow 1–1½ tomatoes, depending on size, per person.

The tomatoes and the dressing can be prepared the day before and left in the fridge covered with clingfilm. The dressing will need a good stir before you use it.

Serves 6

6 tbsp extra-virgin olive oil *for the dressing*
2 tsp Dijon mustard
1 tbsp balsamic vinegar
½ tsp sugar
½ tsp sea salt
a good grinding of black pepper
1 tbsp snipped chives
1 tbsp chopped parsley
several sprigs dill
1 tbsp chopped coriander

assorted salad leaves, arranged on 6 individual plates
9–10 tomatoes, skinned and sliced
1 red onion, skinned and very finely diced

Put all the dressing ingredients into a blender or food-processor and whiz until smooth.

To assemble the salad, arrange the salad leaves on the plates, lay the tomatoes over them and scatter on a small amount of red onion. Spoon or pour the green dressing over the middle of the tomatoes.

cheese sablés

Serves 6

6 oz/175 g Cheddar cheese, grated
6 oz/175 g chilled butter, cut in pieces
6 oz/175 g plain flour
1 tsp mustard powder

Preheat the oven to 400°F/200°C/Gas Mark 6. Put the grated cheese, butter, flour and mustard powder into a food-processor and whiz until the mixture forms a ball. Roll out the dough on a floured surface to a thickness of about ¼ in/0.5 cm, and cut into rounds or triangles. Arrange on a baking tray and bake for 10 minutes. (Set a timer: they burn easily.) Carefully lift the cooked sablés off the tray with a palette knife, and cool on a wire rack. When quite cold, store in an airtight tin.

Baby spinach and sautéed mushroom salad

with Parmesan croûtes

This simple salad can be prepared entirely in advance and takes only seconds to assemble before eating. You will need to sauté the mushrooms until they are almost crisp – this brings out their flavour. You can do this in the morning and they will come to no harm as they cool. The dressing can be made up to a couple of days in advance, and the Parmesan croûtes 3–4 days ahead, providing they are kept in an airtight container.

Serves 6

6 tbsp extra-virgin olive oil *for the dressing*
1 tbsp balsamic vinegar
1 tsp caster sugar
1 tsp sea salt
a good grinding of black pepper
2 tsp Dijon mustard
grated zest of 1 lemon

6 slices thick-sliced white bread, crusts removed *for the Parmesan croûtes*
3 oz/75 g butter, melted
3 oz/75 g freshly grated Parmesan

6 tbsp olive oil
1½ lb/700 g mushrooms, wiped and quartered
6–8 oz/175–225 g baby spinach leaves

Put all of the dressing ingredients into a blender or food-processor and whiz until smooth.

Preheat the oven to 400°F/200°C/Gas Mark 6.

Brush both sides of the bread with melted butter, then cut it into neat ½-in/1-cm dice. Put them on to a baking tray lined with baking parchment, and bake for 20 minutes, turning them once or twice. After 20 minutes they should be golden – give them longer in the oven if not. Take out the tray, scatter the Parmesan evenly over the croûtes, and bake for a further 5 minutes. Take them out of the oven, let them cool completely, and store them in an airtight container.

Heat the olive oil in a large sauté pan, and cook the mushrooms in relays. Don't overfill the pan as the mushrooms will stew rather than sauté crisply. Take them out and let them cool on several thicknesses of absorbent kitchen paper.

To assemble the salad, tear up the spinach and divide it between 6 serving plates. Scatter over the mushrooms, then the Parmesan croûtes. Spoon over the dressing and serve.

Marinated olive and cherry tomato salad

This salad goes well with the Parmesan croûtes on page 125. The olives must be marinated two days before you want to eat them.   **Serves 6**

8 oz/225 g best black olives, Kalamata if possible   *for the olives*
zest of 2 lemons
½ pint/300 ml extra-virgin olive oil
juice of 1 lemon
about 1 tbsp freshly ground pepper, preferably from
4-colour mixed peppercorns
2 tbsp chopped coriander
2 tbsp chopped parsley, flat-leaved

the marinated olives, drained – reserve 3 tbsp of the marinade – stoned and chopped   *for the salad*
1 lb/450 g cherry tomatoes, halved
assorted salad leaves
salt, if you think it is needed

In a jar or other lidded container, stir together the marinade ingredients and the olives. Leave for 2 days.

To assemble the salad, mix together the halved tomatoes and chopped olives, then stir in the salad leaves and the dressing. Divide between 6 plates and serve.

Spicy white bean salad

This salad is much better made with soaked and simmered dried white cannellini beans rather than tinned ones. It depends for its flavour on the best ingredients, notably the olive oil. You can make it entirely the day before it is to be eaten.

Organic stock cubes are available from good supermarkets and health-food shops.

Serves 6

8 oz/225 g dried cannellini beans, soaked overnight in cold water
2 organic vegetable or chicken stock cubes
1 cucumber, peeled, seeded and diced small
3 tomatoes, skinned, seeded and diced
1 small red onion, skinned and very finely diced
2 tbsp chopped flat-leaf parsley

for the dressing
6 tbsp extra-virgin olive oil
1 tbsp balsamic vinegar
zest of 1 lemon
½ tsp sugar
a good grinding of black pepper

Drain the beans and put them into a saucepan with fresh cold water to cover them by 2 in/5 cm. Add the stock cubes, and bring the water to simmering point. Cook the beans gently until they are really tender, and there is no 'bite' to the centre of the bean. This will take at least 1 hour, and you should top up the water in the pan from time to time.

Put the cucumber, tomatoes, red onion and parsley into a bowl, and stir them together well. Mix together the ingredients for the dressing, and stir them into the contents of the bowl.

When the beans are really soft, drain them thoroughly, and stir them while they are hot into the salad – they will absorb the flavours of the rest of the ingredients as they cool. Serve on individual plates – on a bed of assorted leaves, if you like.

Mussels with garlic, white wine and cream

Mussels are so easy – you can buy them anywhere. Look for plump ones, not miserable little specimens. Discard any that are still closed after cooking: the mussel was dead when it was picked, and there is no telling for how long. The creamy parsley and garlic 'soup' means that each guest will need a spoon, as well as a finger bowl. And don't forget a couple more bowls for the shells! This dish must be made and eaten straight away, but it is very quick and easy.

Serves 6

4 lb/1.8 kg mussels
2 tbsp olive oil
4 fat cloves garlic, skinned and finely chopped
½ pint/300 ml water
½ pint/300 ml dry white wine
½ pint/300 ml double cream
4 tbsp chopped parsley, preferably flat-leaf
a good grinding of black pepper
½ tsp salt

Wash the mussels, if they need it – farmed ones often don't. In a very large saucepan with a lid, warm the olive oil over a moderate heat and cook the garlic gently for a couple of minutes. Then tip in the mussels, add the water and wine, cover the pan with its lid and raise the heat. Cook, shaking the pan from time to time, for 5 minutes, or until when you lift the lid you see that the shells have opened. Take the pan off the heat, pour in the cream, then add the parsley and a grinding of pepper. Taste, and add salt only if you think it is needed. Blend the cream well into the liquor at the bottom of the pan – shaking is the best way to achieve this – then ladle the mussels into warmed bowls. Pour over the creamy 'soup' when all the mussels have been dished up. Serve, if you like, with warm bread.

Venison and prune terrine

with Cumberland jelly

This terrine is so convenient: it can be made and kept in the fridge for 2 days before it is needed. In any case, as the venison has to marinate for several hours, you will probably need to start preparation the day before. You could also freeze it ready to cook, but make sure that it is thoroughly thawed before you put it into the oven by sticking your finger into the centre of the raw terrine mixture. Once cooked it doesn't freeze very well – it tastes fine but it crumbles when sliced. You can serve with it any savoury jelly that appeals to you, but I like Cumberland jelly.

Serves 6–8

for the terrine

1½ lb/700 g raw venison, finely diced
8 stoned no-soak prunes, each chopped into 6
3 bay leaves
8 rashers streaky bacon, smoked or unsmoked
1 lb/450 g best-quality pork sausages, skinned

for the marinade

4 tbsp olive oil
¼ pint/150 ml port *or* red wine
1 onion, skinned and finely chopped
a pinch of dried thyme *or* a sprig of fresh thyme, leaves only
pared rind of 1 lemon
½ tsp salt
plenty of freshly ground black pepper
4–5 crushed juniper berries

Put the marinade ingredients into a saucepan and bring it to simmering point. Cook for 3–5 minutes, then take it off the heat and leave it to cool completely. Put the diced venison and prunes into a dish and pour over the marinade. Leave it for several hours in a cool place – overnight if possible.

Preheat the oven to 350°F/180°C/Gas Mark 4. Line a 2 lb/900 g loaf or terrine tin with foil. Lay the bay leaves down the centre. With the blunt side of a knife flatten the bacon rashers and lay them across the tin widthways – their ends will overhang at either side.

Pick out the strips of lemon peel from the marinade. Add the sausages to the marinade and turn them in it so that they are well mixed in. Use your hands to do this. Then pack the mixture into the bacon-lined tin along with the marinade. Fold the overhanging bacon on top of the meat, and cover tightly with foil. Put the tin in a roasting tin with water coming half-way up its sides. Bake for 2 hours. Take the tin out of the oven, and put a weight on top – a couple of tins of baked beans would be ideal. When the terrine is cold take off the weights and store it in the fridge.

To serve, turn it out of the tin and slice it neatly. This terrine is good served with a simple salad made with 6 eating apples, chopped (with the skin left on), and 3 oz/75 g walnuts, dressed with 1 tablespoon olive oil, 2 teaspoons lemon juice, salt and pepper.

Cumberland jelly

2 tsp powdered gelatine
¼ pint/150 ml port
8 oz/225 g redcurrant jelly
1 tbsp Dijon mustard
zest and juice of 1 lemon
zest and juice of 1 orange

Dissolve the gelatine in the port. Put these together with the remaining ingredients into a saucepan and heat gently until the jelly has melted. Pour into warmed sterilized jars and seal.

When cold store in the fridge.

Tagliolini

with white Alba truffle

It is so much easier to buy white truffles these days. I buy mine from Valvona & Crolla in Edinburgh, but many delicatessens stock them. They are such an autumnal treat, and this makes a perfect first course for a special occasion. One large truffle when grated will just about stretch to 3 people. They are expensive but worth it, for their taste and their indescribable, all-pervading fragrance. A whiff of truffle would be agony without the promise of eating it. It is essential to buy the best tagliolini to eat with it. Melted butter, black pepper and grated Parmesan complete this exotic dish. As with the best of everything, it wins through its simplicity.

Serves 6

12 oz/350 g tagliolini
4 oz/110 g butter, melted
2 large white truffles
black pepper
4 oz/110 g Parmesan, grated

Cook the tagliolini until it is *al dente* in plenty of boiling salted water, then drain and immediately stir in the melted butter. Divide it between 6 warmed plates or shallow white bowls, and grate over the white truffles. Serve immediately. Hand the peppermill and grated Parmesan separately.

Twice-baked leek, goat's cheese and walnut soufflé

As with all soufflés, this can be prepared 3–4 hours before you want to cook it, including whisking up the egg whites and folding them into the mixture, providing that you cover the dish with clingfilm. This soufflé combines delicious flavours, and contrasting textures – tell your guests to scrape the base of the dish so that they don't miss the layer of chopped walnuts on the bottom.

Serves 6

3 oz/75 g walnuts, chopped and dry-fried for 3–4 minutes
2 oz/50 g butter
3 medium leeks, trimmed, washed and thinly sliced
2 level tbsp self-raising flour
½ pint/300 ml milk
a grating of nutmeg
a grinding of black pepper
6 oz/175 g creamy goat's cheese, chopped or crumbled small
5 large eggs, separated

Preheat the oven to 425°F/220°C/Gas Mark 7 if you wish to cook the soufflé straight away.

Put the walnuts into the bottom of a buttered 3 pint/1.7 litre soufflé dish. Melt the butter in a saucepan and, over a moderate heat, sauté the sliced leeks till they are very soft – about 5 minutes. Then stir in the flour, and let it cook for a minute or so. Gradually stir in the milk, till the thick sauce bubbles. Season with nutmeg and pepper, take the pan off the heat, and stir in the goat's cheese until it has melted. Beat in the egg yolks, one by one. When the sauce has cooled, whisk the egg whites very stiffly. With a large metal spoon, fold them thoroughly through the soufflé mixture. Pour this into the soufflé dish, over the layer of chopped walnuts. Cover the dish with clingfilm, and leave it in a cool place until you are ready to cook it. If you put it into the fridge, bring it to room temperature 30 minutes beforehand. Bake for 35 minutes, then serve immediately – it should be slightly runny in the middle.

Baked spinach purée with Parmesan

This makes a very good first course or a light lunch. The garlic is optional for those who don't share my passion for it! When I serve it as a main course I put with it a tomato and chilli sauce. I like it warm, but it is good cold too. It is quick to make and cook, and can be prepared in advance.

Serves 6

2 tbsp olive oil
4 x 3 oz/75 g baby spinach
1–2 cloves garlic, skinned and chopped
8 oz/225 g cream cheese, such as Philadelphia
¼ pint/150 ml single cream
1 large egg plus 3 yolks
sea salt
freshly ground black pepper
a grating of nutmeg
3 oz/75 g coarsely grated Parmesan

Preheat the oven to 350°F/180°C/Gas Mark 4.

Heat the olive oil in a large sauté pan with a lid. Cook the spinach in relays in the pan with the lid on, just long enough for it to wilt. Put it into a food-processor and whiz it with the garlic, cream cheese, cream and egg, and add the yolks one at a time. Season with salt, pepper and nutmeg.

Rub a 3 pint/1.7 litre capacity ovenproof dish with olive oil, and scrape the spinach mixture into it. Cover with the Parmesan, and bake until the centre is just firm, about 25–30 minutes. Serve warm, or cold if you prefer.

Leek and bacon timbales

The timbales can be prepared in the morning ready to bake before supper – but give them at least 30 minutes out of the fridge at room temperature before you cook them. Otherwise they will take longer to cook.   **Serves 6**

2–3 oz/56–84 g grated Parmesan
3 tbsp olive oil
4 medium leeks, green part removed, the white trimmed, washed and chopped
2 rashers smoked back bacon, chopped
3 large eggs
¾ pint/420 ml single cream
sea salt
freshly ground black pepper
a grating of nutmeg

Preheat the oven to 350°F/180°C/Gas Mark 4.

Butter 6 ramekins thoroughly – or rub them with olive oil, if you prefer. Dust each with some of the grated Parmesan. Heat the oil in a sauté pan, add the leeks and bacon, and cook over a moderate heat until the leeks are soft. Depending on the size of your sauté pan, this will take 7–10 minutes, but don't let the leeks burn. Take the pan off the heat and let the mixture cool. Purée it in a food-processor until it is smooth, then whiz in the eggs, one by one, and the cream. Taste, and season with salt, pepper, and nutmeg. Divide the mixture between the ramekins, put them into a roasting tin with hot water to a depth of about 1¼ in/3 cm and bake for 30–40 minutes until they feel quite firm in the middle. Take them out of the oven, let them stand for 15 minutes, run a knife around the inside of each ramekin and turn out on to warmed plates. Serve warm.

Creamy fish and shellfish chowder

This is another example of my ideal main course, with everything in one pot. There is absolutely no need for even a salad to go with it: it is full of colour, taste and texture, fish, bacon and vegetables. It is convenient, too, in that part of it – the time-consuming bit – can be done several hours in advance. All that is needed before serving is to heat up the chowder and add the cream and the fish. Use whatever fish and shellfish you like.

Serves 6

3 tbsp extra-virgin olive oil

2 onions, skinned and thinly sliced

4 rashers best back bacon, unsmoked, fat removed, cut into thin strips

2 leeks, trimmed, washed and thinly sliced

8 oz/225 g Jerusalem artichokes, peeled and chopped, *or* 2 extra leeks

1 bulb fennel, trimmed and thinly sliced

4 fairly large potatoes, peeled and cut into neat ½ in/1 cm dice

1½ pints/900 ml vegetable stock

sea salt

freshly ground black pepper

a dash of Tabasco

1 lb/450 g firm-fleshed white fish, such as cod, filleted, and cut into 1½-in/3-cm chunks

1 lb/450 g monkfish, filleted and thickly sliced

12 langoustines, shelled

6 large scallops, cut into 2 or 3 pieces

½ pint/300 ml double cream

6 tomatoes, skinned, seeded and sliced into strips

2 tbsp chopped parsley

Heat the oil in a large saucepan and sauté the onions for about 5 minutes over a moderate heat, stirring occasionally to prevent them sticking. Then add the bacon strips and sliced leeks and the chopped artichokes, and cook for a few more minutes, until the leeks are soft. Scoop the onions, bacon and leeks out of the pan into a warm dish, and put the fennel and the potatoes into the saucepan. Cook for 10 minutes, stirring from time to time. Then return the onions, leeks and bacon to the pan, stir in the stock, salt, pepper and Tabasco, and simmer gently until the potato is soft. Let the saucepan and its contents cool. To serve, reheat the contents of the pan and, when it is simmering gently, add the fish and shellfish. Cook until they are opaque – this will take 5–8 minutes. Then add the cream, bring back to simmering point, taste and adjust the seasoning. Add the tomato strips, and, just before serving in large bowls, add the chopped parsley.

Fillet of hake baked with roasted aubergines

and shallots with aioli

I love hot food with a cold mayonnaise-style accompaniment. Especially, it must be admitted, when there are chips! But even without chips, fish is quite filling and this main course needs only a mixed-leaf salad to go with it. The aubergines, which are among my favourite vegetables, and the shallots can be roasted in advance, but reheat them before you add the fish to them. If you haven't yet developed a passion for chilli leave it out or use less. I love chilli flakes because they are rather hotter than the average fresh chilli. The aioli can be made a day in advance and kept in a bowl covered with clingfilm.

Serves 6

4 large or 5 smaller aubergines, cut into 2-in/5-cm chunks

8 banana shallots, skinned and cut into 2 or 3 pieces, or 24 smaller ones, skinned and left whole

6 tbsp extra-virgin olive oil

1 level tsp dried chilli flakes

sea salt

freshly ground black pepper

6 x 6 oz/175 g filleted hake, skinned

for the aioli

1 whole egg plus 1 yolk

½ tsp caster sugar

about ½ tsp sea salt

a good grinding of black pepper

2 fat garlic cloves, poached for 1 minute, drained and skinned

2 tsp Dijon mustard

½ pint/300 ml extra-virgin and light olive oil combined

1–2 tsp wine vinegar, to taste

2 tsp Tabasco

Preheat the oven to 400°F/200°C/Gas Mark 6.

Line a roasting tin with baking parchment, put in the aubergines and the shallots, with the olive oil and the chilli flakes, and mix them well with your hands, making sure that each piece of vegetable is coated with oil. Spread them evenly, season with salt and pepper, and roast

Roast red pepper, tomato and chilli soup (page 9)

Lime-marinated fresh and smoked salmon in crème fraîche, dill and cucumber, with pink peppercorns (page 15)

Hot-smoked salmon fishcakes with lime and shallot sauce (page 25)

Smoked haddock creamy stew with shallots, saffron and baby spinach (page 29)

Seville orange curd and ginger ice cream with warm dark chocolate sauce (page 46)

Asparagus and saffron risotto (page 74)

Warm chicken salad with chilli croûtes and a parsley dressing (page 80)

Baked aubergines with tomatoes, pesto, black olives and goat's cheese (page 93)

Braised lamb shanks with Puy lentils and pickled lemons (page 147)

Baked bramble and fudge oatmeal and pecan crumble (page 167)

Leek and mushroom salad with toasted pine nuts (page 200)

Marinated marmalade-glazed pork sausages with onion marmalade, and butter-steamed Savoy cabbage (page 220)

for 30–35 minutes, stirring them round from time to time so that they cook evenly. Then take them out and put them into a large sauté pan with a lid.

For the aioli put the egg, the yolk, sugar, salt, pepper, garlic and Dijon mustard into a food-processor. Whiz, adding the olive oil drop by drop initially, then, when you have a smooth and thickening cream, in a steady trickle. Lastly, whiz in the vinegar, tasting after 1 teaspoonful to decide if you need to add more, and the Tabasco. Spoon it either into small individual ramekins, or into one bowl to hand round with the fish and roast vegetables.

Heat the contents of the sauté pan, then press down the pieces of fish into the roast vegetables. Cover the pan with its lid, and cook over a moderate heat for 10–15 minutes – exactly how long depends on the thickness of the fish. Lift the lid and, with a fork, test a piece of fish for doneness: it should fall into flakes.

Herb risotto with smoked haddock

and grilled goat's cheese

Serves 6

A risotto isn't last-minute cooking: it can be made in advance and kept warm, providing that you hold back some stock to finish it off just before serving.

2 lb/900 g smoked haddock, weighed when skinned and filleted,
 cut into 1-in/2.5-cm chunks
5 tbsp olive oil
6 banana shallots, or 12 smaller ones, skinned and finely chopped
1 lb/450 g risotto rice, such as Arborio or Carnaroli
¼ pint/150 ml dry white wine
2 pints/1.2 litres good chicken or vegetable stock
2 tbsp chopped parsley
2 tbsp chopped dill
2 tbsp snipped chives
sea salt
freshly ground black pepper
6 slices goat's cheese – from a 'log' – about 1 cm thick

Prepare the smoked haddock the previous day, if you like, and keep it in a covered bowl in the fridge. Take it into room temperature 30 minutes before cooking it.

Heat the olive oil in a large sauté pan, and cook the shallots until they are soft. Stir in the rice, and cook gently, stirring, so that each grain is coated with oil. Then pour in the wine, and stir as it evaporates. Add the stock, a small amount at a time, stirring occasionally over a moderate heat. Don't let the risotto dry out – it is much better left slightly sloppy.

A few minutes before you are ready to eat, stir in the pieces of smoked haddock and the chopped herbs, taste, season and cook gently for 5 minutes. As you do this, heat the grill, and grill the slices of goat's cheese until they are just bubbling on the surface – goat's cheese browns much more quickly than Cheddar.

Serve the risotto on warmed plates, with a slice of grilled goat's cheese on top of each helping.

Leek and bacon potato cakes

with tomato chilli sauce

Adults and children alike love a savoury 'cake', whether it is a fish cake or, as in this case, a leek and bacon potato cake, which can be put together the day before. Please don't think the chilli in the sauce is obligatory! Leave it out if your passion for chilli isn't on a par with mine.

Serves 6

3 lb/1.35 kg potatoes, weighed when peeled, cooked
½ pint/300 ml milk, warmed
3 oz/75 g butter, diced
sea salt
lots of black pepper
a grating of nutmeg
6 rashers dry-cured back bacon, smoked or unsmoked
4 medium sized leeks, trimmed and washed, if necessary, and sliced finely

2 well beaten eggs *for assembling*
6 oz/175 g white or brown breadcrumbs, on a plate *the leek and*
2 oz/50 g butter *bacon potato*
3 tbsp olive oil *cakes*

Mash the potatoes thoroughly while they are still hot and beat in the warmed milk and the butter. Season with salt, pepper and nutmeg.

Grill the bacon rashers, and when they are cool enough to handle, chop them finely. Tip any bacon fat into a sauté pan – add a tablespoon of olive oil if there isn't enough – and sauté the leeks, stirring occasionally until they are very soft. Let them cool.

Before you start to make up the leek and bacon potato cakes, lay a sheet of baking parchment on a large tray, or on 2 smaller ones. In a bowl, mix the cooled mashed potatoes thoroughly with the cooled leeks and the chopped bacon. Form them into even-sized cakes – if the mixture sticks to your hands, dip them into cold water from time to time as you make the cakes. Dip each cake into the beaten egg then the breadcrumbs. Put them on to the lined trays and leave in the fridge to firm up for several hours, or overnight.

Melt the butter and heat the oil together in a large sauté pan. When it is fairly hot, fry the leek and bacon potato cakes until they are golden brown on both sides. As they are cooked, remove them with a fish slice to a warm dish, containing 2–3 thicknesses of absorbent kitchen paper. They keep warm quite satisfactorily in a low oven before serving.

tomato chilli sauce

This sauce tastes good with the leek and bacon potato cakes, and is a good colour contrast on the plate.

3 tbsp olive oil
2 onions, skinned and finely diced
1 stick celery, strings removed, and very thinly sliced
1–2 cloves garlic, skinned and finely chopped
2 x 14 oz/400 g cans tomatoes
1 tsp dried chilli flakes
½ tsp sugar
1 tsp sea salt
freshly ground black pepper to your taste

Heat the oil in a saucepan and add the onions and celery. Cook for several minutes, until the onion is soft. Then add the garlic, cook for 1 minute, then stir in the tomatoes, chilli, sugar, salt and pepper. Simmer gently for 10 minutes. The sauce can be made, cooled, stored in the fridge and reheated to go with the leek and bacon potato cakes. It keeps for about 3 days, and freezes well.

Potted wild duck

with red onion, orange and mixed-leaf salad

You can use any variety of wild duck for this recipe, or a combination of different ones. If you use teal, double the number of birds in the recipe, which is for mallard.

Serves 6

3 oranges, halved
3 mallard
2 pints/1.2 litres water and red wine mixed – I leave the ratio up to you!
2 onions, halved – skin and all
2 sticks celery
a small handful black peppercorns
1 tsp sea salt

3 oz/75 g butter for clarifying *for the*
the cut-up cooked duck meat *potted duck*
3 tbsp Worcester sauce
juice of 1 orange
3 oz/75 g butter, melted, for the duckmeat
sea salt
freshly ground black pepper, to taste

3 oranges *for the salad*
4 oz/110 g assorted salad leaves
1 small red onion, skinned and very finely diced
3 tbsp extra-virgin olive oil

Preheat the oven to 400°F/200°C/Gas Mark 6.

Put an orange half into each duck and place them in a roasting tin, breast side down, then pour in the water and wine. Add the onions, celery, peppercorns and salt, and cover loosely with baking parchment. Roast for 45–50 minutes. Take the tin out of the oven, and let everything cool.

When it is cold, take the duck out of the tin, and cut all the meat off the carcasses. Throw away the carcasses and the contents of the roasting tin – or strain the liquid and use it for soup.

To make the potted duck, clarify the butter first. Put the butter into a small saucepan on a very, very low heat. Once melted, leave it to stand in a warm place to prevent it solidifying again, but not on direct heat.

Put the duck meat into a food-processor or, if you prefer a rather more textured potted duck (the food-processor tends to pulverize it) dice it very finely with a sharp knife. Put the processed or diced meat into a mixing bowl. Stir in the Worcester sauce, the orange juice, and the other quantity of melted butter. Mix well, taste, and season with salt and pepper. Divide the mixture between 6 ramekins. (If you are using the food-processor, you can combine the ingredients in it but the potted duck will have a pasty consistency.)

Take the pan of melted butter and pour a small amount slowly over the surface of each ramekin. You will find that the milky substance remains in the bottom of the pan.

Leave the potted duck to set, and store it in the fridge, overnight if that is more convenient for you.

To make the salad, take a serrated knife, cut the skin and pith from the oranges, then slice them very thinly, removing any pips you encounter. Arrange them on the salad leaves, scatter over the finely diced onion, then spoon over the olive oil and the orange juice that will have collected during the orange preparation.

Serve with Melba Toast (see page 14).

Pork fillets with apples, onions, cider and cream,

with red cabbage braised with rowanberries

This recipe was a twist on one of mine by our eldest daughter Alexandra. I have to say that her version is rather better than mine! Marinating the strips of pork fillet in milk tenderizes the meat – pat it dry on absorbent kitchen paper before cooking – and this is an excellent way to make the most of our wonderful eating apples in their prime season. I use Cox's or similar eating apples rather than cookers, because I want the apples to hold their shape in slices, rather than collapse into fluffy mush.

Serves 6

2¾ lb/1.25 kg pork fillet, trimmed of membrane and cut into neat finger-thick strips
milk (sufficient to cover the meat in the marinating dish)
3 tbsp olive oil
2 onions, skinned and thinly sliced
4 apples, peeled, cored, sliced and brushed with 2 tbsp lemon juice
1 pint/600 ml dry cider
½ pint/300 ml double cream
sea salt
freshly ground black pepper
a grating of nutmeg

Put the pork fillet into a dish and cover it with milk. Leave it to marinate for at least 2 hours – or even overnight.

Heat the olive oil in a large sauté pan and cook the onions until they are soft and just beginning to colour. Scoop them into a warm bowl, then brown the strips of pork fillet, in relays. Put them into the bowl with the onions. Put the sliced apples into the sauté pan with the cider, and simmer gently until the cider has reduced by about a third, and the apples are soft. Carefully – so as not to break the apple slices – replace the pork and the onions in the sauté pan, and stir them into the cider and apples. Add the cream, and season with salt, pepper and nutmeg. Let the cream bubble for a few minutes, which will slightly thicken the sauce and, at the same time reheat the pork and onions. Serve with the red cabbage, if you like.

red cabbage braised with rowanberries

If you can't get rowanberries, use cranberries instead – they will taste mild in comparison with rowanberries, but not everyone has access to these bitter but useful berries.

Serves 6

2 tbsp olive oil
2 red onions, skinned and thinly sliced
a small handful rowanberries
1 x 2 lb/900 g red cabbage, trimmed and thinly sliced
½ pint/300 ml dry cider
sea salt
freshly ground black pepper

Heat the oil in a sauté pan or a casserole with a lid, and cook the onions until they are soft and starting to caramelize. Add the rowan-berries and the cabbage, and stir everything together well. Pour in the cider, season with salt and pepper, cover with the lid, and simmer very slowly, stirring from time to time, for 30–40 minutes. The cabbage keeps warm satisfactorily, and even freezes well once cooked.

146

Braised lamb shanks

with Puy lentils and pickled lemons

This recipe uses the ingredients for a lamb tagine recipe given to me years ago, but instead of using shoulder of lamb I use lamb shanks, and I include lentils. I love lamb shanks. They are fashionable at the moment, which is usually enough to make me dislike something – but not lamb shanks. I love their flavour; I love the fact that they can be put into the oven and almost forgotten about. They are the most satisfying of autumnal comfort food – well, along with a few other casseroles, steak and kidney pie, and venison pudding! It's important to use pickled lemons for this recipe, and I have included a recipe for them below, but you will need to plan ahead: the lemons take a good three weeks to pickle.

The number of servings a lamb shank provides depends on its size. Those supplied by our butcher feed 2 comfortably.

Serves 6

2–3 tbsp olive oil

3 lamb shanks

12 banana shallots, skinned and halved, or 24 smaller ones skinned and left whole

4 fat cloves garlic, skinned and halved

2 tsp cumin seeds

½ tsp ground cinnamon

12 oz/350 g Puy lentils, washed

2 whole pickled lemons, chopped (see page 148)

1½ pints/900 ml vegetable stock

sea salt

a good grinding of black pepper

Preheat the oven to 250°F/125°C/Gas Mark ½.

Heat a tablespoonful or two of the olive oil in a large casserole and brown the lamb shanks well on all sides. Remove them to a warm dish. Add more olive oil, if needed, and sauté the shallots until they are golden brown. Add the garlic cloves and the spices. Cook for a few minutes, then stir in the lentils and the pickled lemons. Pour in the stock and season with salt and pepper.

Bring the liquid to simmering point, replace the lamb shanks in the casserole, cover with a lid, and cook for 3 hours. Longer won't harm them. Serve with a dish of wilted spinach, if you like, simply dressed with a squeeze of lemon juice and a tablespoon or two of extra-virgin olive oil, salt and pepper.

to pickle lemons

Years ago, when I first wanted to do a recipe that called for pickled lemons, I tried to buy them but couldn't find them anywhere – so I did what I should have done in the first place: I rang the oracle, Clarissa Dickson Wright. Sure enough, with hardly a pause for thought, she told me what to do. And I have made my own pickled lemons – and pickled Seville oranges in their season – like this ever since.

Wash 4 or 5 lemons well. Have ready a large jar – ideally a Kilner jar. Cut through each lemon as if you were cutting it into quarters, but don't cut through the base of the lemon – you will have a sort of tulip effect. Put the lemon into the jar then put as much of 1 tablespoon of sea salt into it. Continue with the other lemons until the jar is full, then pour boiling water over the lemons to the top of the jar, seal it with a tightly fitting lid, and don't open it for 3–4 weeks. After that, the pickled lemons will keep in their jar for up to a year, so long as they are in the fridge.

Lamb and chorizo chilli

This can be made a couple of days in advance – in fact it tastes even better if you do this and reheat it before serving. Warm garlic bread goes down well with this!

Lamb shoulder is sweeter than leg, and therefore better with the spices in this recipe.

Serves 6

6 tbsp olive oil

2¾ lb/1.25 kg shoulder lamb, weighed when trimmed of fat, cut into ¾-in/2-cm chunks

1 lb/450 g chorizo, skinned and cut into ¾-in/2-cm chunks

3 onions, skinned and sliced

2 fat cloves garlic, skinned and chopped

3 bird's eye chillis, seeded and chopped, *or* 1½ tsp dried chilli flakes

zest of 1 lemon

1 tsp ground cinnamon

1 tsp cumin seeds

1 level tbsp flour

2 pints/1.2 litres vegetable stock

8 oz/225 g dried kidney beans, soaked overnight, rinsed, then simmered for 1 hour

sea salt

freshly ground black pepper to taste

2 tbsp chopped coriander leaves

½ pint/300 ml *crème fraîche* or soured cream, to garnish

Preheat the oven to 350°F/180°C/Gas Mark 4.

Heat the oil in a large sauté pan with a lid, or in a heavy casserole. Brown the lamb and the chorizo, a small amount at a time, over a high heat. Remove it with a slotted spoon, to allow excess oil to drip back into the pan, and put it on to a large warmed dish.

Lower the heat a little, and add the onions. Sauté them, stirring occasionally, until they are soft, then add the garlic, chilli and lemon zest. Sauté for a further couple of minutes. Add the cinnamon and cumin, continue to cook for a minute, then stir in the flour. Cook for another minute then pour in the stock, stirring until everything comes to a gentle simmering point. Replace the browned meat in the pan and add the drained kidney beans. Season with salt and pepper. Stir until the liquid is just simmering again, cover the pan with its lid, and put it into the oven for 1 hour. Take it out and let it cool. Reheat, from room temperature, on the hob to simmering point then put it into the oven at 350°F/180°C/Gas Mark 4 for a further 30 minutes. Push a fork into a piece of meat – it should feel tender. If it doesn't, continue to cook for a further 15 minutes.

Just before serving, stir in the chopped coriander. When you dish up, dollop a spoonful of *crème fraîche* or soured cream on each helping. Serve with a mixed-leaf salad, or warm, wilted spinach.

Braised lamb with aubergines, red peppers, potatoes

and chilli with garlic and coriander

This is another of those invaluable dishes where everything is in one pot. I have two large sauté pans, made by Berndes, with domed Pyrex lids and detachable handles, and they are perfect for cooking this and so many other dishes. Otherwise use a heavy flameproof and ovenproof casserole with a wide base.

This benefits from being made a day in advance, which allows all the flavours to blend together.

Serves 6

2 lb/900 g lamb, weighed when trimmed, preferably shoulder
8 tbsp olive oil
1½ lb/700 g potatoes, either scrubbed or peeled, and cut into ¼-in/5-mm dice
2 red onions, skinned and thinly sliced
2 medium aubergines, diced as the potatoes
2 red peppers, halved, seeded and cut into thin strips
1 mild fresh green chilli, halved, seeded and finely chopped
sea salt
3–4 tomatoes, skinned and chopped
freshly ground black pepper
6 cloves garlic, skinned and chopped
1 tbsp sweet paprika
1 tbsp cumin seeds
1 tbsp chopped parsley
2 tbsp chopped coriander
3 tbsp lemon juice

Cut the lamb into chunks approximately ¾ in/2 cm. In a large sauté pan heat 3 tablespoons of the olive oil. Brown the lamb thoroughly, and remove it to a warm dish. Add the potatoes and cook them for about 10 minutes, until they are turning brown at the edges. Take them out and keep them warm while you sauté the onions and the aubergines until soft. (Alternatively, you can toss the aubergines in olive oil and roast them with the onions in the oven until they are soft.) Return the potatoes and the lamb to the pan, add the pepper strips and the chilli, then season with salt and sauté for a further

5 minutes. Add ½ pint/300 ml water, cover the pan with its lid, and shake it. Turn down the heat to a gentle simmer and braise until the vegetables are soft, stirring from time to time. Add the tomatoes 5 minutes before you are ready to serve the dish.

Meanwhile, make the sauce. Take either a pestle and mortar or a food-processor and smash the garlic cloves to a paste with some salt, paprika and cumin seeds. Add the parsley and coriander – this is easiest done in a food-processor if you haven't already chopped the herbs – then the rest of the olive oil and the lemon juice. If any liquid remains in the sauté pan with the vegetables and lamb, remove the lid and boil it off. Stir in the sauce mixture, coating all the vegetables and pieces of meat in the sauté pan thoroughly. Taste, season with pepper, and add more salt or lemon juice if you think it is needed. Serve.

Pot-roast rabbit with root vegetables

Oven-ready rabbits are easier and easier to buy, but if you don't like rabbit substitute organic chicken. A pot-roast is so easy, must be prepared well in advance of eating, and almost everything is in the one pot. All that is required to go with this dish are baked jacket potatoes.

Serves 6

6 tbsp olive oil
6 x 6 oz/175 g rabbit (or chicken) joints
6 banana shallots, skinned and halved, or 12 smaller ones, skinned and left whole
4 fat cloves garlic, skinned and halved
3 carrots, peeled and cut into chunks
3 parsnips, peeled and cut into chunks
3 medium leeks, trimmed, washed and thickly sliced
8 oz/225 g Jerusalem artichokes or swede, peeled and halved, if large
sea salt
freshly ground black pepper
1 pint/600 ml chicken stock

Preheat the oven to 350°F/180°C/Gas Mark 4.

Heat the oil in a large casserole, and brown the rabbit joints well on both sides. Remove them to a warm dish. Then sauté the shallots until they are beginning to turn colour. Add the garlic and the rest of the prepared vegetables to the casserole. Stir everything around in the hot oil for a couple of minutes. Season with salt and a good grinding of pepper. Push the browned rabbit joints down among the vegetables and pour in the stock. Cover the casserole with its lid, and put it into the oven for 45 minutes, then lower the heat to 250°F/125°C/Gas Mark ½ and continue to cook for a further 45 minutes. The meat will be falling from the bones.

Marinated steaks with pepper cream sauce

and roast root vegetables

This is a trouble-free main course: the steaks need only to be lifted out of their marinade, patted dry and cooked just before you want to eat them. The pepper sauce can be made ahead and reheated, while the vegetables can be put in to roast 2 hours before dinner, then transferred to a warmed serving dish and kept in a low-temperature oven until needed. You can use any combination of root vegetables, but I always include some shallots among them.

Serves 6

10 tbsp extra-virgin olive oil
2 fat cloves garlic, skinned and sliced
1 tbsp coarsely ground black pepper
6 x 6–8 oz/175–225 g best fillet steaks

for the roast root vegetables

3 carrots, peeled and cut into 2-in/5-cm chunks
3 parsnips, peeled and cut to the same size as the carrots
6 banana shallots, skinned and halved, or 12 smaller ones, skinned and left whole
3 beetroot, peeled and cut into chunks
½ turnip or swede, peeled and cut into chunks
6 tbsp olive oil
2 tsp sea salt

for the sauce

1 tbsp coarsely ground black pepper
1 pint/600 ml double cream
2 tsp lemon juice

Mix the olive oil, garlic and pepper together, and spoon it over the fillet steaks in a wide, shallow dish. Leave for several hours in a cool place. Turn the steaks once during their marinating time.

Prepare the root vegetables. Preheat the oven to 400°F/200°C/Gas Mark 6. Line a large roasting tin with baking parchment.

Put the prepared vegetables into the tin, pour over the olive oil and mix everything together well with your hands. Spread the vegetables evenly in the tin, scatter over the salt, and roast for 45-55 minutes, moving the vegetables around from time to time so that they cook evenly. Transfer to a warmed serving dish.

autumn main courses

Make the sauce simply by putting the pepper into a saucepan over a moderate heat. Cook, shaking the pan a bit, for 5–7 minutes, to toast it. Then add the cream, and simmer gently until it has thickened. Stir in the lemon juice just before serving.

To cook the steaks depends on what you like to cook them on or in. I have a ridged griddle, which I use on the hot Aga plate. I heat this well, before I put the steaks on, and cook them according to the taste of the people who are going to eat them: allow 1½ minutes each side for medium-cooked steaks. Whatever you cook your steaks on, it's a mistake to move them around too much as they cook. Once mine are on the griddle, I leave them alone until it is time to turn them over.

Serve, with the sauce spooned half over each steak.

Venison fillet

with wild mushroom sauce

We buy wild venison saddles, and trim the fillet from them. This makes an elegant main course as well as a quick one, although it needs fairly last-minute cooking. The venison can be trimmed of all membrane, ready to sear in the sauté pan. The accompanying sauce can be made in advance and reheated to serve with the venison. The wild mushroom content will depend on what you can get – you can use just one type, say, chanterelles, or a combination of several. Wild mushrooms and venison seem to have been made for each other: they go so well together.

With this main course, in which the sauce is almost an accompanying vegetable in itself, I like to serve a purée of root vegetables, smooth and silky with cream, garnished with butter-fried cashew nuts for a contrasting crunch.

Serves 6

for the sauce

4 tbsp olive oil, perhaps more
3 banana shallots, or 6 smaller ones, skinned and finely diced
2 lb/900 g wild mushrooms, chopped
1 pint/600 ml red wine, such as Merlot
½ pint/300 ml double cream
sea salt
freshly ground black pepper

2 lb/900 g trimmed venison fillet
olive oil
sea salt
freshly ground black pepper

First make the sauce: heat the olive oil in a sauté pan and cook the shallots for 2–3 minutes over a moderate heat. Scoop them into a warmed bowl, turn up the heat and sauté the wild mushrooms – you should do this in relays, and may need more olive oil than I have suggested above. Cook them until they are very well done – this will enhance their flavour – then scoop them into a separate warm dish. Replace the shallots in the sauté pan, and add the wine. Simmer until it has reduced by about two-thirds – the shallots absorb the flavour of the wine as it reduces. Then return the mushrooms to the pan, add the cream, taste and season with salt and pepper. Simmer gently until the sauce thickens.

To cook the venison, heat the olive oil in a large sauté pan with some salt and a good grinding of black pepper. Don't season the meat itself: this encourages the juices to run from it. When the oil is very hot, seal the fillets well on all sides: the meat will be rare in the middle. If you would prefer to eat it pink rather than red, roast the seared fillets at 425°F/220°C/Gas Mark 7 for 10 minutes. Leave the meat to rest (while you eat your first course) to let the juices settle, then slice it, and serve it with the wild mushroom sauce spooned around it, or if you prefer, handed separately.

Chunky three-cheese tart

with Parmesan pastry and pear and redcurrant sauce

We have been serving a different version of a Three-cheese Tart for many years at Kinloch as a first course. This is last year's variation and we have made it like this ever since. The cheeses are diced into 1-in/2.5-cm chunks, which melt as the tart bakes but to some extent retain their shape. It makes for interesting eating – another example of my enthusiasm for contrasting textures. We use Isle of Mull Cheddar, a blue cheese, such as Stilton or Dunsyre Blue, and a creamy cheese, usually a Bonchester Brie. Leave the rind on the Brie but remove it from the blue cheese and the Cheddar.

You can make the pastry case up to a week ahead, but keep it in an air-tight container.

Serves 6

for the pastry
5 oz/150 g plain flour
2 oz/50 g freshly grated Parmesan
4 oz/110 g butter, hard from the fridge, diced

for the filling
4–5 oz/110–150 g each blue cheese (such as Stilton), Cheddar and Brie, each cut into 1-in/2.5-cm chunks
½ pint/300 ml single cream
a good dash Tabasco
2 large eggs and 2 yolks, beaten together
plenty of black pepper

for the sauce
1 jar (1 lb/450 g) redcurrant jelly
3 Conference pears, peeled, cored and chopped
½ pint/300 ml port

To make the pastry, put the flour and Parmesan into the food-processor with the butter and whiz until the mixture resembles fine crumbs. Pat and press this firmly around the sides and base of a 9-in/23-cm flan dish or tin – if you use a tin, make sure it has a removable base and that it is sufficiently deep. Put it into the fridge for at least 1 hour. Preheat the oven to 350°F/180°C/Gas Mark 4 and bake for 20 minutes, or until the pastry is pale golden, then take it out and allow to cool. Don't turn the oven off.

Distribute the three cheeses over the pastry base, mixing them up well. Beat the cream and the Tabasco into the eggs with plenty of pepper. Pour it carefully among the pieces of cheese. Bake for 15–20 minutes until the filling no longer wobbles in the centre when you gently shake the flan dish.

To make the sauce, melt the redcurrant jelly over a gentle heat. Put the chopped pears into a food-processor or blender, and whiz with the melted jelly and the port.

Serve the tart with the sauce, either cold or warm, and a mixed-leaf salad.

Garlic croustade

with leeks, Brie and pine nuts

This is one of Kath Stevenson's inventions, and it is so good that we make it regularly. You can use whichever cheese you like in the filling, but I particularly enjoy the leek and Brie combination. The croustade base can be made a day in advance, providing that once it is cold you cover it closely with clingfilm.

Serves 6

for the croustade

10 oz/275 g brown breadcrumbs
1–2 cloves garlic, to taste, skinned and very finely chopped
3 oz/75 g butter, melted
½ tsp sea salt
a good grinding of black pepper

for the filling

2 tbsp olive oil
6 medium leeks, trimmed, washed and thinly sliced diagonally
8 oz/225 g Brie, edge rind cut off, the top and bottom left on, sliced into thin strips
1 large egg and 2 yolks
½ pint/300 ml single cream
½ tsp sea salt
freshly ground black pepper
a grating of nutmeg
3 oz/75 g pine nuts

Preheat the oven to 350°F/180°C/Gas Mark 4.

Mix together the croustade ingredients thoroughly, then press firmly around the sides and base of a 9-in/23-cm flan dish. Bake for 20–25 minutes, or until the crust is toasted in appearance. Let it cool. Don't turn off the oven.

Make the filling. Heat the oil in a sauté pan and cook the sliced leeks until they are soft, about 3–5 minutes. Let them cool, then spoon them over the base of the cooled croustade. Arrange the slices of Brie among them.

In a bowl, beat together the egg and the yolks, gradually adding the cream. Season with salt, pepper and nutmeg, and pour this over the leeks and the Brie. Scatter over the pine nuts. Bake until the centre of the filling no longer wobbles when you gently shake the flan dish. Serve warm, rather than hot from the oven.

Baked pasta au gratin – mark two

This is completely different from the recipe of the same title in the spring collection (see page 38)! It is just as convenient, though, because it can be made in the morning, ready to bake in time for supper. This has fried chopped walnuts as a lovely crunchy top, with Taleggio for the cheese, and roasted vegetables. All that is needed by way of an accompaniment is a
Serves 6 *mixed-leaf salad.*

4 red onions, skinned and thinly sliced
3 large aubergines, cut into neat 1-in/2.5-cm dice
2 cloves garlic, skinned and finely chopped, optional
4 courgettes, thinly sliced
6 tbsp olive oil
sea salt
2 sprigs thyme, about 4 in/10 cm long
freshly ground black pepper
18 oz/500 g short pasta, such as penne or fusilli
12 best black olives, stoned and chopped
6 tomatoes, skinned, seeded, halved, each half sliced into 4 strips
1 lb/450 g Taleggio, rind removed and cut into small chunks
½ pint/300 ml double cream

for the walnut 2 oz/56 g butter
top or crust 1 tsp sea salt
4 oz/112 g chopped walnuts

Preheat the oven to 400°F/200°C/Gas Mark 6.

Line a large roasting tin with baking parchment – this makes washing-up easier – and cover it with a thin layer of the onions, aubergines, garlic and courgettes – don't mound them up, it's better to do them in two batches, or the inside of the mound will steam rather than roast. Mix in 3 tablespoons of the olive oil to coat the vegetables – do this with your hands. Scatter about 2 teaspoons of salt over the surface, and the thyme sprigs and black pepper, and roast for 35–40 minutes, stirring the outer vegetables towards the middle twice during the cooking time. If after the cooking time they still look underdone, continue to roast for another 10 minutes.

When you are ready to assemble the gratin, bring to the boil a saucepan full of water, with 1 teaspoon of salt, add the pasta, bring the water back to the boil, and cook for 4–7 minutes, until the pasta is *al dente* – when you stick your thumbnail (clean!) into it there should still be a slight bite to it. Drain the pasta well, then mix in the remaining 3 tablespoons of olive oil.

Rub the inside of a large ovenproof dish with olive oil. Mix together the pasta, the olives and the tomatoes. Add the cheese and toss it in with your hands. In an oiled ovenproof dish arrange the roast vegetables and the pasta and tomato mixture in layers, ending up with a layer of vegetables. Pour in the cream.

To prepare the walnut topping, melt the butter in a sauté pan and add the salt. Add the chopped nuts and stir-fry them until they are a darker brown. Cool on several thicknesses of absorbent kitchen paper.

Scatter the fried walnuts over the surface of the gratin and bake at 350°F/180°C/Gas Mark 4 for 30–35 minutes.

Honey-glazed baked apples stuffed with

dates and raisins marinated in ginger wine and orange

The dates and raisins can be marinated up to 2 days in advance. The cooking apples take only a couple of minutes to prepare, and I make the most of them while they are in season. Scoring around their middles prevents them bursting while they are in the oven.

Serves 6

6 oz/175 g dates, stoned and chopped
6 oz/175 g best-quality raisins, for example, Lexia
4 tbsp ginger wine
zest and juice of 2 oranges
7 large cooking apples – one extra in case of mishap
7 tbsp thick honey

for serving
½ pint/300 ml *crème fraîche*
6 pieces of stem ginger, drained and chopped

Mix the dates and raisins with the ginger wine, the orange zest and juice. Leave for several hours, or overnight.

Preheat the oven to 325°F/165°C/Gas Mark 3. Put a sheet of baking parchment on a baking tray. Wash and dry each apple, and remove the core – feel inside to make sure you have removed all of the tough bits. Score them around the middle – the equator. Drain the marinated fruit, and divide it between the apples, pushing the fruit down well to pack it into the hole left by the core. Spoon honey over each apple, and bake for 15–20 minutes, or until the apples feel soft when you gently press the sides. Combine the ginger with the *crème fraîche*. Serve warm, with the ginger *crème fraîche*.

autumn puddings

Orange-glazed apple and vanilla tart

with lemon and orange pastry

This tart has a refreshing filling in a rich, buttery, crisp, flavoursome pastry, which can be made several days in advance, providing that it is kept in an air-tight tin. The tart can be filled and baked in the morning. Any left over will be delicious the next day, but it is at its best eaten on the day it is made.

Serves 6–8

4 oz/110 g butter, hard from the fridge, diced *for the pastry*
6 oz/175 g plain flour
1 oz/25 g icing sugar
zest of 1 lemon and 1 orange

1 x 1lb/450 g pot shredless marmalade, either orange or lemon, whichever you prefer *for the filling*
4 oz/110 g butter
2 whole eggs plus 2 large egg yolks, beaten together
a few drops vanilla extract
6 good eating apples, Cox's or similar, peeled, cored, sliced and brushed with lemon juice

Whiz the pastry ingredients in a food-processor until they are the texture of fine crumbs. Pat and press them firmly around the sides and base of a 9-in/23-cm deep flan dish or tin, and put it into the fridge for at least 1 hour. Preheat the oven to 350°F/180°C/Gas Mark 4, and bake for 20 minutes, or until the pastry is pale golden.

To make the filling, put the marmalade into a Pyrex bowl with the butter, and put the bowl over a saucepan of simmering water. Stir until both the butter and the marmalade have melted. Then take the bowl off the heat and stir in the beaten eggs with the vanilla extract. Arrange the apple slices over the pastry, and carefully pour in the buttery marmalade mixture. Return to the oven for 15 minutes, then shake the tart gently: if it wobbles in the middle, put it back for another few minutes until it is just set in the centre. Take it out and serve it warm or cold.

Bramble and blueberry compote

with almond and lemon biscuits

Blueberries are acknowledged to be a healthy fruit as they are allegedly packed with antioxidants. I love them anyway, raw or cooked, but when blueberries are cooked their identity changes. Raw, they have a dusky bloom and are delicious but mild in flavour. Cook them and the bloom vanishes, the taste sharpens, and they need sweetening. I love the crispness of these biscuits with the soft fruit.

Serves 6

for the compote

1 lb/450 g each brambles and blueberries
zest and juice of 1 lemon
½ pint/300 ml water
3 oz/75 g sugar, caster or granulated
1 cinnamon stick

To make the compote, put the berries into a saucepan with the other ingredients. Over a low to moderate heat stir until the sugar has dissolved, then simmer gently for 5 minutes. Take the pan off the heat, and let the compote cool. Pour it into a serving bowl.

almond and lemon biscuits

Makes 12–16

4 oz/110 g butter
4 oz/110 g caster sugar
1 tbsp golden syrup
6 oz/175 g self-raising flour, sieved
½ tsp bicarbonate of soda
3 oz/75 g flaked almonds
zest of 2 lemons

To make the biscuits, preheat the oven to 350°F/180°C/Gas Mark 4.
  Cream the butter and sugar until pale and fluffy, then beat in the golden syrup, followed by the flour and bicarbonate of soda. Stir in the almonds and lemon zest, then roll the dough into even walnut-size balls. Put them on a greased baking tray and bake for 13–15 minutes until golden. Lift them off with a palette knife and let them cool on a wire rack.

autumn puddings

Baked bramble and fudge oatmeal

and pecan crumble

This crumble top contains no flour and is a delicious combination of pinhead oatmeal (if you can't find this, rolled porridge oats are a second-best substitute), chopped pecans or walnuts, in a fudgy butter and sugar mixture. If you have a surfeit of brambles, use twice the amount and leave out the blueberries, but I love both fruit combined. You can make the entire pudding and reheat it to serve the day after it is made.

Serves 6

2 lb/900 g brambles and blueberries mixed
2 tbsp cold water
2–3 oz/50–75 g sugar

6 oz/175 g butter   *for the crumble*
8 oz/225 g pinhead oatmeal
6 oz/175 g pecans or walnuts, chopped
6 oz/175 g Demerara sugar
1 tsp vanilla essence, *or* ½ tsp extract

Stew the fruit over a low heat with the water and sugar until the juices run. Pour the contents of the saucepan into a 4–5-pint/2.2–2.7-litre ovenproof dish.

Preheat the oven to 350°F/180°C/Gas Mark 4.

To make the crumble, melt the butter in a large sauté pan and fry the oatmeal and the chopped nuts until the oatmeal looks slightly toasted. Then stir in the Demerara sugar and the vanilla. Cook for a few more minutes, stirring, then spoon this mixture evenly over the cooked brambles. Bake for 25–35 minutes, or until the top is sizzling gently and the surface is quite darkly golden brown. Serve warm or cold, with *crème fraîche*, whipped cream or vanilla ice cream.

Baked damson and lemon pudding

If you live where true damsons grow you are fortunate indeed. When I say true damsons, I have seen small plums sold as damsons that weren't the damsons I love. Small, intensely flavoured damsons make the best jam in the world, and some of the best fruit-based puddings. They freeze well, raw or cooked. But if you can't get them, use a good cooking plum instead – a sweet eating plum, like the Victoria, becomes bland when it is cooked.

Serves 6

1½ lb/700 g damsons
6 tbsp water
2 tbsp caster sugar

3 oz/75 g butter
8 oz/225 g caster sugar
zest of 3 lemons
juice of 2 lemons
6 large eggs, separated
2 oz/50 g flour, sieved
½ pint/300 ml milk

Stew the damsons in the water until their skins just burst, then stir in the sugar. Lift the damsons out with a slotted spoon, and, with a fork, pick out the stones. Put the damsons into a 4-pint/2.2-litre oven-proof dish.

Preheat the oven to 350°F/180°C/Gas Mark 4. Cream the butter and sugar until the mixture is light and fluffy. Beat in the lemon zest, then the juice. Beat in the egg yolks one by one. If the mixture curdles, don't worry – it doesn't affect the end result. Beat in the sieved flour, and, lastly, the milk.

Whisk the egg whites until they are very stiff. Then, with a large metal spoon, fold them thoroughly into the lemon mixture – this is a fairly sloppy batter, but again, don't worry, all will be well. Pour the mixture over the damsons and bake for 45–50 minutes. Half-way

autumn puddings

through the cooking time rest a piece of baking parchment lightly on top of the pudding to stop it becoming too brown.

The pudding will separate while it cooks to form a light sponge on top with a thick lemon custard among the damsons. I like it best served warm, with whipped cream or *crème fraîche*.

Caramelized pineapple

with caramelized pistachio nuts

Serves 6

You can serve this warm or cold, and it is most refreshing. If you don't like nuts, leave them out.

2 medium pineapples, or 3, if they are small
4 oz/110 g butter
4 oz/110 g Demerara sugar

for the nuts   **2 oz/50 g butter**
3 oz/75 g granulated sugar
6 oz/175 g shelled pistachios, chopped

With a serrated knife, slice the skin off the pineapples, and cut off both ends. Nick out the little brown indentations. Quarter the pineapples and remove the cores. Cut each quarter in half, and then into bite-size uniform dice.

Melt the butter in a large sauté pan, and add the sugar. Stir it in well, then put in the pineapple and cook, stirring occasionally, for 5 minutes. The pineapple juice will blend with the sugary butter. Transfer the pineapple and the juice to a serving bowl or dish.

Now prepare the nuts. Melt the butter in a sauté pan and stir in the sugar. Add the nuts, and cook over a moderate heat, shaking the pan so that they don't burn, for several minutes. When the nuts are bubbling and browned, spoon them over the pineapple in its serving dish.

Pear, almond and vanilla clafoutis

A warm pudding is so welcome on a cold evening, and this one makes the most of our autumnal pears. You can use any type of pear, but I think that a ripe Conference pear is hard to beat. You can make the lovely rich vanilla-scented clafoutis batter in advance, and also prepare the pears, providing you brush them with lemon juice and keep them closely covered with clingfilm, to prevent discoloration.

Serves 6

6 ripe medium pears or 3 larger ones
juice of 1 lemon
3 oz/75 g plain flour
4 oz/110 g caster sugar
3 large eggs
¾ pint/450 ml single cream
2 oz/50 g melted butter
1 tsp vanilla essence, *or* **½ tsp vanilla extract**
4 oz/110 g flaked almonds, dry-fried until they are toasted

Preheat the oven to 350°F/180°C/Gas Mark 4. Butter thoroughly a 5-pint/2.7-litre fairly shallow ovenproof dish.

Peel, halve and core the pears. Slice each half into 3 or 4. Put the slices into the base of the buttered dish and brush them with lemon juice.

Make the batter: sieve the flour and sugar into a bowl, make a well in the middle and break the eggs into it. With a metal whisk, incorporate the eggs with the flour, as you gradually pour in the cream, then the melted butter and the vanilla. Whisk until you have a smooth batter. Alternatively put all the ingredients into a food-processor and whiz until smooth.

Pour the batter over the pears, scatter the surface with the almonds, and bake for 35–40 minutes, or until the pudding is puffed up and darkly golden brown. It should be cooked through – push a sharp knife point in the middle to test and it should come out clean. Serve warm, with whipped cream or thick *crème fraîche*, if you like.

Spiced panna cotta

with marinated raisins in apple purée

This is a yummy combination of complementary tastes and textures. The apple purée can be made 2–3 days in advance then kept in the fridge, and the raisins marinated for up to 2 days – but it is the quality of the raisins you use that will elevate this pud to dizzy heights. We buy half-dried grapes, from our excellent supplier Caledonian Foods – truly the most delicious raisins I have ever tasted – and their half-dried apricots, too, which are sublime. In the absence of such Rolls-Royce raisins, though, buy Lexia, which were the best

Serves 6 *until I tasted the half-dried grapes!*

for the apple purée with marinated raisins

3 oz/75 g best raisins, for example, Lexia

4 tbsp Calvados

2 lb/900 g Bramley apples, weighed when peeled and cored, then chopped

2 tbsp water

3 tbsp soft brown sugar

zest of 1 lemon and 1 orange

for the panna cotta

3 leaves gelatine *or* 1½ tsp powdered gelatine

1½ pints/900 ml single cream

1 vanilla pod, split

1 cinnamon stick

3 oz/75 g caster sugar

about 5 gratings of nutmeg

To prepare the marinated raisins in apple purée, mix together the raisins and Calvados – or any other *eau-de-vie* – and leave for a minimum of 6 hours or up to 2 days.

Put the apples into a saucepan with the water, sugar, lemon and orange zest, cover the pan, and cook over a medium heat, stirring occasionally, until the apples fall to a pulp. Stir well to smooth the purée. Take the pan off the heat, and stir in the marinated raisins with any marinade that they haven't soaked up. Leave to cool.

To make the panna cotta, set the gelatine to soak: if you are using leaves, put them in a bowl of water; if you are using powdered, put it into a bowl with 2 tablespoons of water. Put the cream into a saucepan with the vanilla pod and the cinnamon stick. Heat it until it forms a skin, don't let it boil, then take the pan off the heat and leave it to cool. Scrape down the vanilla pod so that the seeds are mixed into the cream. Reheat, with the sugar and nutmeg, stirring until the sugar has dissolved. Throw away the cinnamon stick, and remove the vanilla pod – if it is a fresh one, wash it well so that you can use it once more.

Stir the soaked gelatine into the hot cream until it has melted completely. Pour the cream into 6 glasses, and leave it to cool.

Serve the apple purée to accompany the panna cotta, or spooned on top of it if the glasses are large enough.

Hazelnut meringue

with chocolate and apple purée

In this pudding the meringue is made with ground hazelnuts and the chocolate is in the whipped cream filling. The surface is dusted with a mixture of icing sugar and cocoa powder. The meringues can be made several days in advance and stored in an airtight container. The puréed apples will keep in the fridge for up to 3 days.

Serves 6–8

for the meringue

4 large egg whites

8oz/225 g caster sugar

1 tsp white wine vinegar

1 tsp vanilla essence *or* ½ **tsp extract**

4 oz/110 g ground hazelnuts, toasted until golden, then cooled

for the filling and decoration

½ pint/300 ml double cream

½ pint/300 ml apple purée

6 oz/175 g best-quality dark chocolate, coarsely grated

2 tsp icing sugar

2 tsp cocoa powder

Preheat the oven to 350°F/180°C/Gas Mark 4.

To make the meringue, put the egg whites into a clean bowl and whisk until they are stiff. Then, whisk in the caster sugar a spoonful at a time, until it is all incorporated and you have a stiff meringue. Add the vinegar and vanilla essence, and fold them in with the ground hazelnuts using a large metal spoon.

Divide the meringue mixture between two 8-in/20-cm sandwich cake tins, the bases lined with non-stick baking parchment. Smooth the tops and bake for 30 minutes. Take the meringues out, leave them in the tins for 5 minutes, then turn out carefully on to a wire rack to cool. They will have a crusty surface that may crack and crumble a bit but don't worry.

To make the filling, whip the cream stiffly and reserve a third of it. Carefully fold the apple purée and the chocolate into the bulk of the cream. About an hour before serving, spread it over the top of one of the meringue rounds. Cover with the second. Tip the icing sugar and the cocoa powder into a sieve together, and sieve over the surface. Pipe rosettes of the remaining whipped cream at intervals round the edges of the plate. Use a serrated knife dipped into a jug of very hot water to cut it.

Hazelnut roulade

with vanilla crème pâtissière and brambles

This makes the most of the seasonal hazelnuts and brambles. I dry-fry the coarse-ground nuts rather than grilling them. When the telephone rings, you automatically pull a sauté pan of nuts off the heat before you go to answer it. The same can't be said of the grill pan as I know to my own cost! This roulade can be made in the morning for eating that evening – the juice of the brambles seeps into the crème if it is made a day in advance. But if it is more convenient, make the roulade anyway, fill it with the vanilla crème and the whipped cream, then roll it up, cover it closely with clingfilm, and serve the brambles as an accompanying compote.

Serves 6

for the filling
1 lb/450 g brambles
5 oz/150 g caster sugar
½ pint/300 ml single cream
1 tsp vanilla essence *or* **½ tsp vanilla extract** *or* **1 vanilla pod, split**
3 large egg yolks
½ pint/300 ml double cream, whipped

for the roulade
4 large eggs, separated
4 oz/110 g caster sugar
a pinch of salt
2 oz/50 g coarse-ground hazelnuts, toasted and cooled
icing sugar, sieved

Stew the brambles with 2 oz/50 g of the caster sugar until their juices run, then set them aside to cool.

Now make the vanilla *crème pâtissière*. Put the single cream into a saucepan with the split vanilla pod, if you are using it, but not the extract or essence, and, over a moderate heat, bring it to scalding point. Meanwhile, beat together the yolks and the rest of the sugar, then stir in the hot cream, mixing well. Either cook the cream mixture in a Pyrex bowl set over a saucepan of simmering water, stirring until it is very thick or, quicker, put the mixture into a Pyrex bowl, with the vanilla pod, if you are using one, and into a microwave

autumn puddings

oven on high for 1 minute. Take the bowl out, whisk the cream, then return it to the microwave for another 30 seconds on medium. Take the bowl out, whisk the contents, and repeat, on medium for 30 seconds at a time, until the cream is thick. This should take about 4 minutes. (Scrape the seeds from the vanilla pod into the cream, then, if the pod is a fresh one, wash it thoroughly to re-use it once more.) If you are using essence or extract, add it to the cream now. Leave it to cool.

To make the roulade, preheat the oven to 350°F/180°C/Gas Mark 4. Line a shallow baking tray or a swiss-roll tin with baking parchment, securing it in each corner with a dab of butter under the paper. In a bowl whisk the egg yolks with the caster sugar until they are very thick and pale. In a separate bowl, whisk the egg whites with the salt. Fold the hazelnuts with a large metal spoon into the egg mixture, then fold in the whisked whites thoroughly so that there are no little pockets of egg white. Pour it over the surface of the lined baking tray and smooth it even. Bake for 15–20 minutes, until the roulade feels firm to the touch. Take it out of the oven, cover with a cloth and leave it to cool.

To roll it up, put a large sheet of baking parchment on a work surface, and dust it liberally with the icing sugar. Tip the roulade still in the tin face down on to this, and carefully peel the paper off the back of the roulade. Fold the vanilla *crème pâtissière* into the whipped cream, and spread it over the surface. With a slotted spoon, lift the brambles from their juice, letting them drip as much juice back into the container as you can, and cover the cream with them. Roll up the roulade, lengthways, using the baking parchment to guide you, then slip it on to a serving plate. To serve, slice thickly.

Baked dark and white chocolate cheesecake

This is a truly scrumptious pud. You can make the pastry case 2–3 days in advance, providing that you cover it tightly with clingfilm when it has cooled, or wrap it in foil. Bake the cheesecake in the morning to eat that evening. I don't use much white chocolate, but if you buy the best – ours is made by Callebaut – it can be very good in a pudding like this. To grate the dark chocolate, hold it in a double thickness of foil to prevent the heat of your hand melting it.

Serves 6

for the pastry base

4 oz/110 g butter, hard from the fridge, diced

5 oz/150 g flour

1 tbsp icing sugar

a few drops vanilla extract

for the filling

4 oz/110 g white chocolate, broken up

2 tbsp water

8 oz/225 g cream cheese, such as Philadelphia

3 oz/75 g caster sugar

2 large eggs

a few drops vanilla extract *or* ½ **tsp essence**

4 oz/110 g dark chocolate, grated

Preheat the oven to 350°F/180°C/Gas Mark 4.

Put the ingredients for the pastry base into a food-processor. Whiz until the mixture resembles fine crumbs, then press it firmly around the sides and base of a 9-in/23-cm flan dish or tin. Put it into the fridge for at least 1 hour. Bake for 20 minutes, or until the pastry is lightly biscuit-coloured. If the sides slip down the sides of the flan dish, press them up again with the back of a metal spoon. Bake for a further few minutes. Don't turn the oven off if you plan to bake the cheesecake straight away.

To make the filling, put the white chocolate with the water into a Pyrex bowl and set it over a saucepan of barely simmering water. Let the chocolate melt gently – white chocolate is even more temperamental to melt than dark, so don't try to hurry it. Put the cream cheese and the caster sugar into a food-processor and whiz, adding the eggs, one at a time. Add the melted white chocolate and the vanilla, then whiz until it is all smoothly blended. Stir in the grated dark chocolate – you don't want to pulverize this, so just tip it into the food-processor and stir with a rubber spatula. Scrape the mixture into the pastry case, and put it into the oven for about 25 minutes, until the filling is just firm in the middle. It will continue to cook for a little longer when you take it out of the oven. Serve cold or warm.

Toasted coconut and vanilla sponge pudding

with dark chocolate sauce

Some people turn up their noses at the very thought of desiccated coconut, but many are converted when they taste it toasted – dry-fry it, shaking it in a sauté pan over a moderate heat until it changes colour ... and flavour. Toasted coconut goes awfully well with vanilla and dark chocolate, and all three flavours are combined in this pudding.

Serves 6

6 oz/175 g butter

6 oz/175 g caster sugar

3 large eggs

6 oz/175 g self-raising flour, sieved

2–3 tbsp milk

2 tsp vanilla essence *or* 1 tsp vanilla extract

½ pint/300 ml double cream

1 tbsp sieved icing sugar

3 oz/75 g desiccated coconut, toasted

1 quantity Warm Dark Chocolate Sauce (see page 56)

Preheat the oven to 350°F/180°C/Gas Mark 4. Line a 9-in/23-cm cake tin with a baking-parchment disc. If it isn't a non-stick tin, butter and flour the sides first.

Cream the butter, gradually adding the sugar, until the mixture is light and fluffy. Beat in the eggs, one at a time, alternating with spoonfuls of flour. Beat in a small amount of milk if the mixture becomes too stiff: the mixture should drop from the spoon. Beat in 1 teaspoon of the vanilla essence or ½ teaspoon of the extract, then pour the cake mixture into the tin and smooth the top. Bake for 20–25 minutes, or until a skewer pushed into the centre comes out clean. Let the cake cool on a wire rack, then peel off the baking parchment.

To assemble the pudding, whip the cream with the icing sugar and the remaining vanilla until it holds soft peaks. Put the cake on a serving plate and cover the top with the vanilla cream, then cover this with the toasted coconut – some will inevitably fall around the cake on its plate, but I think this looks attractive. Serve in slices, with the Warm Dark Chocolate Sauce handed separately. You could serve a fruit compote with the cake instead of the chocolate sauce.

Baked dark chocolate puddings

Serves 4

4 oz/110 g butter
4 oz/110 g dark chocolate
2 large whole eggs
2 large egg yolks
2 oz/50 g caster sugar
2 tsp self-raising flour, sieved

Preheat the oven to 420°F/220°C/Gas Mark 7. Butter 4 ramekins and dust them with sieved flour.

Put the butter and the chocolate into a Pyrex bowl over a pan of simmering water and let them melt together, stirring until they have combined smoothly.

Whisk together the whole eggs, the yolks and the caster sugar, until the mixture is very thick and pale. Stir the melted chocolate and butter into the egg mixture then, carefully and quickly, fold in the sieved flour. Divide this between the 4 prepared ramekins, put them on a baking tray and bake for 9–10 minutes.

Serve with chilled vanilla-flavoured, slightly sweetened whipped cream, or with a good vanilla ice cream.

Dark chocolate and pecan tart

A particularly good tart to round off a special occasion dinner. The toffee part is in the fudgey filling. Pecans are such good nuts, with no bitterness about them, and are much easier to buy than they used to be. If you feel they need refreshing before you cook them, dry-fry them in a sauté pan, shaking it, for a few minutes.

Serves 6

3 oz/75 g plain flour   *for the pastry*
4 oz/110 g pecan nuts
4 oz/110 g butter, hard from the fridge
a few drops vanilla extract
2 tbsp Demerara sugar

¼ pt/150 ml double cream   *for the toffee*
4 oz/110 g granulated sugar
4 oz/110 g butter

½ pint/300 ml double cream   *for the*
8 oz/225 g best dark chocolate, broken into small pieces   *chocolate cream*

Preheat the oven to 350°F/180°C/Gas Mark 4. Butter a 9-in/23-cm flan dish.

Put the pastry ingredients into a food-processor and whiz until the mixture resembles coarse crumbs. Press this firmly around the sides and base of the flan dish, then put it into the fridge for at least 1 hour. Bake for 20 minutes, or until the nutty pastry base is just beginning to come away from the sides of the dish. Leave it to cool.

Put the toffee ingredients into a saucepan over a moderate heat and stir until the butter has melted and the sugar dissolved, and there is no gritty sensation beneath your wooden spoon as you stir. Let the mixture simmer for 5 minutes. Pour it over the tart base. Leave it to cool.

Now make the chocolate cream. Put the cream into a saucepan and heat it. When it is hot, turn off the heat, put in the chocolate and stir until it has melted in the heat of the cream. Pour this into the tart over the toffee and leave to set.

If you should have any problems cutting this tart – you shouldn't – dip a knife into a jug of very hot water between slices.

Pistachio ice cream

Not the lurid green stripe of yesteryear in Wall's Neapolitan but the real thing. **Serves 6–8**

6 large egg yolks
2 oz/50 g caster sugar
1 pint/600 ml single cream, scalded with a split vanilla pod
½ pint/300 ml double cream, whipped to soft peaks
2 large egg whites
2 oz/50 g icing sugar, sieved
4 oz/110 g pistachio nuts, crushed and dry-fried to refresh but not toast them

Beat the yolks well with the caster sugar until well mixed, then pour on some of the scalded cream. Scrape the seeds from the vanilla pod into the cream, then if it is a fresh one, wash it, to use once more. Stir the egg mixture into the rest of the vanilla-flavoured cream, then either stir it in a Pyrex bowl set over a pan of simmering water until it thickens sufficiently to coat the back of your wooden spoon, or cook it in the microwave: in a Pyrex bowl, give it 30 seconds on high, beat well, then repeat on medium for 30 seconds, beat well, and continue thus until the sauce has thickened. Let it cool completely.

Fold the whipped cream into the vanilla custard. Whisk the egg whites, and when they are stiff gradually whisk in the icing sugar, continuing to whisk till you have a stiff meringue. With a large metal spoon, fold this and the pistachios into the creamy mixture. Pour it into a solid polythene container and put it into the freezer. Bring the ice cream into room temperature for 30 minutes before serving, or put it into the fridge 1½ hours beforehand.

Serve either on its own or with Warm Dark Chocolate Sauce (see page 56) – yum.

My only complaint about winter is that we don't get enough frost and snow in Skye. I love winter, and nowhere on earth could be more beautiful than Skye in snow. I love the short days, and being able to draw the curtains in mid-afternoon against the dark skies, and, theoretically, sitting beside the fire to eat a huge tea. That's my idea of bliss, but not what I actually put into practice – apart from once or twice – each winter. That is what our hotel guests do, though, and that is what I would want to do were I on holiday in Skye. Of course, Christmas is in the middle of winter, and for me Christmas is the high spot of the whole year. And I have come to love New Year, too – any excuse for a party! – but Christmas is so special because our family comes home.

I love the food we eat during December, January and February – the meaty stews and casseroles, thick soups and winter salads. The winter menus (see page 265) are simplicity itself and sometimes the main courses consist of just one dish. There are menus, too, for more formal occasions – especially the last one in the section – but formal food need not mean frenzied last-minute kitchen activity. There is even a menu for a picnic: a picnic on a clear, cold winter's day is great fun, providing you build a bonfire and pack lots of warming food.

The dishes in this section reflect what is available in its natural season in the UK. The prime example is the plethora of root vegetables. The same goes for venison, game in the form of pheasant, and winter fruits such as clementines and cranberries. Several dishes contain no meat or fish. The most important thing, though, is for food to be sustaining in the winter, with the maximum potential for enjoyment both in the eating and the preparation.

Sweet potato, lime and ginger soup

Serves 6

You can substitute another root vegetable for the sweet potato in this soup – or try a combination: carrots, parsnips, celeriac and Jerusalem artichokes are all nearly as good with the ginger and lime as the sweet potato.

3 tbsp olive oil
2 onions, skinned and chopped
about 2 in/5 cm fresh root ginger, skinned and chopped
1 clove garlic, skinned and chopped (optional)
4 sweet potatoes, peeled and chopped
1½–2 pints/900–1.1 litres best chicken or vegetable stock
zest and juice of 2 limes
8 fl oz/225 ml full-fat *crème fraîche*
sea salt
freshly ground black pepper
a grating of nutmeg

Heat the oil in a large saucepan and cook the onions for several minutes until they are soft and translucent. Add the ginger and the garlic and cook for a further couple of minutes. Then add the sweet potatoes and cook for 10 minutes or so, stirring occasionally to prevent them sticking and to make sure that they cook evenly. The longer you cook the sweet potatoes at this point the better the end result will be. Stir in the stock and add the lime zest. Half cover the pan with a lid, and simmer gently until the pieces of sweet potato are quite soft when pressed against the sides of the pan with a wooden spoon. When the soup has cooled a little, liquidize it with the lime juice and the *crème fraîche*. Return it to the pan to reheat. Taste, and season with salt, pepper and nutmeg.

winter first courses

Leek and chicken soup

with blanched lemon peel

The excellence or otherwise of this soup depends on the quality of the chicken stock you use. It is a convenient first course, because it can be made entirely in advance – indeed, the stock may have been frozen. All you need do is reheat it before serving.

Serves 6

2 pints/1.2 litres best chicken stock (see page 192)
2 large egg whites
a pinch of salt
2 lemons, rind pared and sliced into thin strips
4 medium-sized leeks, trimmed, washed and very thinly sliced
sea salt
freshly ground white pepper if possible, but black if not
(it can look like dead midges in clear soup . . .)
2 tbsp medium or dry sherry, optional

Put the stock into a large saucepan and heat it. Meanwhile, whisk the egg whites with the pinch of salt until they are stiff. When the stock is boiling, whisk in the egg whites: they will form a covering over the stock and absorb all the shreds of vegetable and chicken from it to clarify it. After about 15 minutes of simmering, strain the stock through a large sieve lined with a double thickness of absorbent kitchen paper.

Meanwhile, bring a saucepan of water to boiling point, and add the lemon strips and the leeks. Simmer, gently, for 15–20 minutes. Test a bit of leek: it should be very soft. Drain the leeks and lemon rind. Pour the strained stock into a clean saucepan. Add the leeks and lemon rind, and reheat. Taste, and season with salt and pepper. Add the sherry, if you are using it, just before serving the soup.

chicken stock

2 raw chicken carcasses
3 onions, halved, with skin
a head of celery, washed and roughly chopped
2–3 leeks, washed and chopped
1 tbsp black peppercorns
2 bay leaves
2 tsp sea salt

Put all of the above ingredients into a stockpot and cover with cold water – 6–7 pints/3.3–3.8 litres. Bring it to boiling point, then turn down the heat and simmer gently for about 5 minutes. Cover the pan with a lid, and leave it overnight in a slow oven, 250°F/125°C/Gas Mark ½ (I put the stock, once simmering well, in the top left oven of my 4-door Aga). The longer the cooking time the better.

When the stock has cooled, strain it, remove the fat and either use it or freeze it. It seems to take up so much less room in the freezer if it is frozen in plastic mineral water or lemonade bottles.

Baked Brie, with an almond and Demerara sugar crust

served with grape salsa

I first ate Baked Brie cooked by Lucy Lister Kaye, years and years ago. It was handed round with drinks, and it was so good I wanted to disappear with it and eat the lot. I serve it for family and friends as a first course, with this slightly fiery grape salsa and good oatcakes or warm bread. Any leftover Brie heats up well for eating the following day.

You must buy a whole Brie, but smaller ones are easy to find. You can prepare it hours before baking it, and the salsa should be made ahead, too, to give the flavours time to settle down together.

Serves 6

1 small Brie, measuring about 8 in/20 cm in diameter
3 oz/75 g flaked almonds
1 tbsp Demerara sugar
½ tsp sea salt

1 lb/450 g seedless grapes, halved *for the*
1 small red onion, skinned and finely diced *grape salsa*
2 sticks celery, stringy bits removed, sliced thinly
2 tbsp chopped parsley, flat-leaf if possible
grated zest of 1 lime
3 tbsp extra-virgin olive oil
2 tsp balsamic vinegar
1 tsp Tabasco
½ tsp sea salt
freshly ground black pepper

First make the salsa: put the grapes, onion, celery and parsley into a bowl, and mix in the lime zest, olive oil, balsamic vinegar, Tabasco, salt and pepper. Mix thoroughly, and leave until you are ready to hand it round with the baked Brie. The salsa tastes better if it is made several hours in advance, because the flavours have a chance to blend together.

Preheat the oven to 350°F/180°C/Gas Mark 4.

With a sharp knife slice the top off the Brie, taking care not to take any cheese with the skin. Mix together the almonds, sugar and salt, and scatter over the surface. Bake the Brie either in its wooden box or on a heatproof dish – a ceramic flan dish is ideal – for 20–25 minutes, until it is bubbling slightly and the almonds are golden brown. Serve as soon as you can.

Potted cheese with watercress and red onion salad

with walnut dressing

I love this either as a first course, or as a main course for lunch or supper, with a bowl of soup. Use the best Cheddar, which for me is from the Isle of Mull. The potted cheese won't suffer if it is made as much as three days in advance, but cover the ramekins with clingfilm to prevent the surface drying out.

Serves 6

12 oz/350 g Cheddar, grated
½ pint/300 ml single cream
1 tbsp Dijon mustard
1 level tsp Patum Peperium – Gentleman's Relish
plenty of black pepper
a grating of nutmeg

for the potted cheese

6 tbsp extra-virgin olive oil
3 oz/75 g chopped walnuts
2 tsp balsamic vinegar
½ tsp caster sugar
½ tsp sea salt
black pepper
juice of 1 orange
6 oz/175 g watercress, picked over and torn into easy-to-eat bits
½ red onion, skinned and very thinly sliced

for the watercress and red onion salad with walnut dressing

Put the cheese into a saucepan and add the cream, mustard, Patum Peperium, pepper and nutmeg. Over a low heat, melt the cheese in the single cream and, when all is smooth, either pour into a bowl, or divide it between 6 ramekins. Cool, and leave in a cold place, the larder or fridge.

Warm the olive oil in a sauté pan and add the chopped walnuts. Cook them gently for several minutes. Stir in the balsamic vinegar, the sugar, salt, pepper and orange juice and mix well. Pour the dressing into a bowl and let it cool. Put the watercress and red onion into a salad bowl. Just before serving, pour over the dressing and toss well.

Serve the potted cheese and salad with toast or warmed bread.

Smoked salmon with Avruga crème fraîche

Buy the best smoked salmon you can find – I love the fairly delicate smoked salmon we buy from the Summer Isles Smokehouse at Achiltibuie, but I also love the stronger one from Craster Smokehouse, in Northumberland. Good smoked salmon is still the delicacy it should be but there is a lot of inferior stuff around. Avruga is lightly smoked herring roe and is fairly widely available. We served this as a first course at our daughter Isabella's wedding in November 2000.

Serves 6

2 x 4.2 oz/120 g size jars Avruga
½ pint/300 ml best full-fat *crème fraîche*
plenty of freshly ground black pepper
12 oz/350 g smoked salmon
1 large lemon, cut into 6 wedges

Mix together the Avruga and the *crème fraîche*, and season well with black pepper. Arrange the smoked salmon on 6 plates, with a good spoonful of the Avruga *crème fraîche* beside it. Put a wedge of lemon on each plate.

Serve with thinly sliced and buttered brown bread.

Orange, mint and olive salad

with cumin dressing

This is a perfect first course to serve before any fairly filling main course. **Serves 6**

for the dressing

1 tsp cumin seeds, crushed in a pestle and mortar
4 tbsp extra-virgin olive oil
3 tsp balsamic vinegar
½ tsp caster sugar
½ tsp sea salt
freshly ground black pepper

about 24 large best-quality green or black, or mixed, olives,
stoned and chopped
a handful of mint leaves – at this time of year it has to be spearmint, chopped
assorted salad leaves
6 oranges, peel and pith removed with a sharp serrated knife, very thinly
sliced, pips removed

Put all the dressing ingredients into a screw-topped jar and shake it
vigorously to mix everything well.

Put the olives and mint into a bowl, and pour over the dressing.
Mix well. Arrange the salad leaves on 6 plates and lay on them the
sliced oranges. Spoon over the olives and mint with the dressing.

Watercress, pink grapefruit and red onion salad

with vinaigrette

I know that in these days of plenty we shouldn't need to calculate the vitamin content of what we eat, but it's no bad thing to keep an awareness of such things at the back of our minds. Watercress is so high in vitamin C and iron that it is a very useful salad vegetable to eat regularly throughout the winter. In this simple salad it is combined with pink grapefruit segments and a small amount of red onion.

Serves 6

for the dressing

6 tbsp extra-virgin olive oil
2 tbsp balsamic vinegar
$\frac{1}{2}$ tsp caster sugar
1 tsp sea salt
a good grinding of black pepper
chopped parsley, flat-leaf if possible, to garnish

3 pink grapefruit
$\frac{1}{2}$ red onion, skinned and very finely diced
6 oz/175 g watercress, torn into easy-to-eat bits

Make the dressing by shaking all the ingredients together in a securely screw-topped jar.

Slice the peel from the grapefruit with a sharp, serrated knife, cutting away all the white pith. Slice towards the centre of each fruit on either side of the tough white membranes that encase each segment. Put the segments free of membrane into a bowl. Mix the finely diced red onion thoroughly into the grapefruit segments. Arrange the watercress on 6 plates, spoon the grapefruit and red onion over it, and dress with a good spoonful of the vinaigrette. If you like, serve cheese sablés with this salad, or warm bread rolls.

Marinated figs and rocket salad

with grilled goat's cheese

We are lucky to be able to buy huge plump succulent dried figs. A health-food shop is one of the best sources for such ingredients. This recipe can be prepared hours before or, better still, the day before it is to be eaten, apart from grilling the goat's cheese. The sweet sharpness of the fig marinade is delicious with the cheese.

Serves 6

1 lb/450 g best-quality dried figs, diced or cut into 4 pieces (scissors dipped in hot water are the easiest way to cut the figs)
6 x ¾-in/2 cm slices goat's cheese
6 oz/175 g rocket

6 tbsp extra-virgin olive oil
2 tsp balsamic vinegar
finely grated zest and juice of 2 oranges
1 tsp sea salt
a good grinding of black pepper
2 tbsp snipped chives

for the marinade and dressing

Put the diced figs into a bowl. Mix together the ingredients for the marinade, and pour it over the figs. Stir thoroughly, and leave for several hours, or overnight.

Shortly before you plan to eat, lay the goat's cheese slices on a baking tray lined with lightly oiled foil. Heat the grill to red-hot and cook the goat's cheese until the surface bubbles, about 1 minute.

Mix the marinated figs with the rocket, and divide it between 6 plates. Put a slice of grilled goat's cheese on each, and serve with some warm bread if you like.

Leek and mushroom salad

with toasted pine nuts

Any winter salad is convenient, particularly if it consists of cooked vegetables. I like to steam the leeks. If they are boiled it is almost impossible to drain off the water – a certain amount becomes irrevocably trapped within the leaves. Leeks and well-sautéed mushrooms combine well together, and the toasted pine nuts add a lovely contrasting texture.

Serves 6

9 medium leeks, trimmed, washed and sliced diagonally into 3
about 4 tbsp olive oil
1½ lb/700 g mushrooms, wiped and quartered
4 oz/110 g pine nuts
assorted salad leaves

for the dressing

4 tbsp extra-virgin olive oil
1 tbsp balsamic vinegar
1 tsp caster sugar
zest of 1 lemon
½ tsp sea salt
a good grinding of black pepper
1 tbsp chopped parsley, preferably flat-leaf

Steam the sliced leeks until they are tender.

Meanwhile, pour the dressing ingredients into a screw-topped jar and shake well.

Heat the olive oil in a large sauté or frying-pan and cook the mushrooms in relays, so that they don't stew. Sauté them until they are almost crisp, and remove them to a warm plate. Let them cool.

When the leeks are ready, put them into a wide dish and spoon over the dressing. Leave them to cool.

Toast the pine nuts to a light golden brown.

To assemble the salad, divide the leaves between 6 plates, and spoon over them the leeks in their dressing. Distribute the sautéd, cooled mushrooms over the leeks, and scatter on the toasted pine nuts.

Beetroot remoulade

Beetroot is the unsung hero of our delicious root vegetables, which are in season throughout the late autumn, winter and early spring. In its raw state it looks eminently unspectacular, but peeled and either cooked or coarsely grated and eaten raw, it is wonderful. It isn't just superb in colour – an almost ecclesiastical hue – it has such a distinctive and delicious flavour. In this first course, it is partially cooked then mixed into a Dijon mustard mayonnaise. The mayonnaise can be made 2–3 days in advance and kept in the fridge. The beetroot can be parboiled a day ahead and kept covered in the fridge. Take both the mayonnaise and the beetroot into room temperature for an hour before serving.

Serves 6

1½ lb/700 g raw beetroot, weighed when peeled
assorted salad leaves

1 whole egg and 1 egg yolk *for the dressing*
2 tsp Dijon mustard
½ tsp caster sugar
½ tsp sea salt
a good grinding of black pepper
½ pint/300 ml light olive oil
2 tsp white wine vinegar
a small handful of dill

Either coarse-grate the peeled beetroot, or slice it into very thin julienne, using a mandolin. Don't worry about your stained fingers, they will soon wash clean!

Put the egg, the yolk, the mustard, sugar, salt and pepper into a food-processor and whiz, adding the olive oil drop by drop initially, then in a thin, steady trickle. When it is all used up, whiz in the wine vinegar and the dill. Scrape the mayonnaise into a bowl.

Meanwhile, bring a saucepan of water to boiling point, and plunge in the beetroot. Turn down the heat and simmer for 3–4 minutes, then drain, running cold water through the beetroot to cool it and refresh its colour. Pat it dry with kitchen paper. Mix the cooled beetroot into the mustard and dill mayonnaise – it will become purple-streaked.

Divide the salad leaves between 6 plates, then the beetroot. I don't think any garnish is necessary, except perhaps a frond of dill on each serving.

Spicy courgette fritters

with tomato and chive mayonnaise

These chilli-spiced courgette fritters are far more convenient to make than you might imagine. The courgettes and garlic can be sautéd and mixed into the batter well in advance of frying the fritters. The accompanying mayonnaise can be made a day or two ahead and kept in the fridge. I love a mayonnaise, of whatever flavour, with hot food, and here is a perfect example.

Serves 6

1 large egg and 1 egg yolk	*for the tomato and chive mayonnaise*
1 tsp Dijon mustard	
½ tsp caster sugar	
1 tsp sea salt	
a good grinding of black pepper	
½ pint/300 ml extra-virgin olive oil	
1 tbsp balsamic vinegar	
3 tomatoes, skinned, seeded and diced small	
about 1 tbsp snipped chives	

4–5 tbsp olive oil, plus extra for cooking the fritters	*for the courgettes*
6 small to medium courgettes, diced to about the size of a little fingernail	
1–2 cloves garlic, skinned and finely chopped	
½ tsp dried chilli flakes	
½ tsp sea salt	

6 oz/175 g plain flour	*for the batter*
1½ tsp baking powder	
½ tsp sea salt	
a good grinding of black pepper	
just less than ½ pint/300 ml milk	
1 large egg	

First make the mayonnaise. Put the egg, the yolk, the mustard, sugar, salt and pepper into a food-processor and whiz. Add the olive oil, drop by drop initially, then in a steady trickle, until all the oil has been used and you have a thick mayonnaise – if it is too thick, whiz in a tablespoon or two of near boiling water to thin it a little. Whiz in the balsamic vinegar, then scrape the mayonnaise into a serving bowl. Stir in the diced tomatoes and the snipped chives. Keep the mayonnaise covered, in the fridge, until you are ready to serve it with the fritters.

Heat the olive oil in a large sauté pan and cook the diced courgettes, mixed with the garlic, chilli and salt, stirring until they are lightly golden brown and soft.

Mix together the batter ingredients and beat well. Stir in the cooked courgettes, chilli and garlic.

To cook the fritters, heat some olive oil in a sauté pan and drop spoonfuls of the courgette mixture into the hot oil. Make 2 fritters per person, not too large. Cook for a couple of minutes on each side until they are golden brown. Remove them to a warm dish lined with a double thickness of absorbent kitchen paper and keep them warm. Serve with the mayonnaise.

Baked butternut squash, onion

and parsnip au gratin

This is such a good first course, substantial, full of flavour, easy to eat, and convenient to make. It can be made ahead up to the final baking. You can substitute any root vegetables for the butternut squash and parsnips, but three-quarters cook whichever vegetables you use before baking: carrots in particular take much longer to cook.

Serves 6

2 butternut squash, peeled, seeded and diced to thumbnail size
6 medium parsnips, 5 if they are large, 8 if they are small, peeled and cut into neat matchsticks
3 tbsp olive oil
2 medium onions, skinned and thinly sliced
1 rounded tsp medium-strength curry powder
sea salt
freshly ground black pepper
½ pint/300 ml double cream
2 oz/50 g breadcrumbs, white or brown
2 oz/50 g butter, melted
2 tbsp chopped parsley

Preheat the oven to 350°F/180°C/Gas Mark 4.

Put the squash and the parsnips into a steamer and steam them until tender. Take them off the heat. Heat the oil in a large sauté pan and cook the onions, stirring from time to time, until they are beginning to caramelize. Stir in the curry powder half-way through. When the onions are colouring, add the steamed squash and parsnips to the pan. Stir carefully, so as not to break up the vegetables, and season with salt and plenty of pepper.

Oil a 4-pint/2.2-litre ovenproof dish: it should be wide and shallow rather than narrow and deep. Put the contents of the sauté pan into the dish. Pour in the cream. In a bowl mix together the breadcrumbs, melted butter and parsley, and scatter over the cream and vegetables. Bake for 30–40 minutes, or until the top is golden brown and crispy.

It will keep warm satisfactorily for 30 minutes before serving.

Eggs Benedict

This is a classic dish, invented in Brennan's restaurant in New Orleans, and it is a perfect combination of crispness, in the toasted buttered muffins, and flavour, in the slice of ham under the poached egg and the Hollandaise. But, there are one or two points to bear in mind: the ham must be of the very best quality, boiled or baked; and the Hollandaise sauce must not be too bland. I always make mine flavoured with reduced wine vinegar, and prefer the result to Hollandaise made with lemon juice. Also, it must be good and thick, and in sufficient quantity! The eggs can be poached before you start dinner and kept in a bowl of warm water – not hot, as they will continue to cook. The muffins can be split, toasted, buttered and kept warm, and the Hollandaise made up to an hour in advance, and kept warm.

Serves 6

for the Hollandaise sauce

6 egg yolks

12 oz/350 g butter, cut into 12 pieces

about 4 tbsp reduced, flavoured wine vinegar (see page 207)

12 eggs, poached, and slipped into a large bowl of warm water

6 muffins, split in half, toasted, then buttered

12 slices best ham, fat trimmed off

To make the Hollandaise, beat the egg yolks in a Pyrex bowl, then set the bowl over a saucepan containing simmering water, and stir in the butter, a piece at a time, until it has all gone in and you have a thick, glossy sauce. Warm the vinegar, and whisk in 3 tablespoons, taste, and if you like it sharper (I do) whisk in the fourth spoonful. Take the bowl off the pan of water, and keep it in a warm place – at the back of an Aga or Raeburn is ideal, if you have one.

To assemble, put 2 toasted and buttered muffin halves on each warm plate. Cover each half-muffin with a slice of ham. Lift the poached eggs from their warm bath, pat them dry with absorbent kitchen paper, and put an egg on each slice of ham. Coat with Hollandaise, and serve immediately.

to reduce wine vinegar

I do a bottle of white wine vinegar at a time so that I always have some in reserve.

1 bottle white wine vinegar
½ onion, skinned and cut into 3
a bay leaf
a handful of crushed parsley stalks
about 12 black peppercorns
stick of celery

Put all the above ingredients into a saucepan and boil until the vinegar has reduced by half. Cool, strain into a jug, and pour the cooled flavoured vinegar back into the bottle or into a screw-topped jar. Store in the fridge, and use as required.

Scallops with Jerusalem artichokes and leeks

This simple main course is very filling – all shellfish are, and scallops are no exception. You will know the appetites of those you are feeding, but I allow 3–4 large (king) scallops per person as a main course, when there has been a first course and there is to be a pud to follow. The scallops take little cooking, but the artichokes and leeks need much longer and can be sautéed then baked well in advance, and warmed up to mix with the scallops. You can, if you like, spoon them on to a small mound of assorted salad leaves, and serve this main course as a warm salad. The leaves wilt slightly under the warmth of the cooked ingredients. Leave out the chilli if you really don't like it, but I find more and more people do. It is addictive!

Serves 6

4 tbsp olive oil

4 oz/110 g butter

6 medium leeks, trimmed, washed and thickly sliced on the diagonal

1½ lb/700 g Jerusalem artichokes, weighed when peeled, cut in half if large

1 fat red chilli, halved, seeded and chopped

sea salt

freshly ground black pepper

3–4 large king scallops per person, the ridge of white muscle at the side removed

juice of 1 lemon

about 6 oz/175 g assorted salad leaves

Heat the oil and half of the butter in a large sauté pan with a lid. Put in the leeks and the artichokes, and stir them around to coat each piece in the buttery oil. Add the chilli, and season with salt and pepper. Cover the pan with its lid, and cook slowly over a gentle heat until the artichokes are almost falling to mush. Then, in a separate sauté pan, melt the remaining butter and cook the scallops briefly, for 35–40 seconds, then turn them and cook on their other side for the same length of time. They should be opaque right through. Lift them into the pan with the leeks and artichokes, and stir them in with the lemon juice.

To serve, either put them on warm plates and pass the salad separately, or, as I mentioned earlier, divide the leaves between 6 warm plates and spoon the scallops, leeks and artichokes over the top.

Hot-smoked salmon kedgeree

with quails' eggs and saffron

Here is another main course in which everything is in one dish. You could accompany this kedgeree with a simple leaf salad, but nothing else is required. The best hot-smoked salmon is sold by Salar, in South Uist. It is so lightly cooked that in this kedgeree it doesn't take on the cardboard texture (and taste) that salmon assumes when overcooked. The kedgeree can be made and frozen without the quails' eggs – add them when you reheat it.

Serves 6

1 smoked haddock fillet *for the stock*
1 onion, skinned and halved
2½ pints/1.4 litres milk and water mixed, half and half

2 tbsp olive oil *for the kedgeree*
1 oz/25 g butter
4 banana shallots, or 8 smaller ones, skinned and finely chopped
12 oz/350 g long-grain rice – I use Basmati
2 good pinches saffron strands
1½ lb/700 g hot-smoked salmon, flaked, skin removed
2–3 tbsp chopped parsley, flat-leaf preferably
12 quails' eggs, hard-boiled, shelled and halved
lots of freshly ground black pepper
3 oz/75 g butter, diced

Make the stock first. Put the smoked haddock, onion, milk and water into a saucepan over a moderate heat, and bring the liquid to simmering point. Take the pan off the heat and leave it to cool completely. Strain into a jug.

In a large sauté pan, or saucepan with a lid, heat the oil and butter together. Put in the chopped shallots and sauté until they are very soft and translucent. Add the rice, and stir for 2–3 minutes, so that each grain is coated in buttery oil, and is very well mixed with the shallots. Add the saffron. Pour in the strained smoked-haddock stock until it comes to about 1 in/2.5 cm above the level of the rice in the pan. When you first add the liquid there will be a whoosh of steam: wait until this subsides to see the depth of liquid. Once the liquid has been added to the pan don't stir. Replace the pan on the heat, cover it with a tea-towel (which will absorb the steam) and the lid, and cook over a gentle heat for 5 minutes. Take the pan off the heat and leave it for 15 minutes (still covered). By this time the liquid should have been absorbed by the rice, and the rice should be cooked.

With a fork, so as not to break up the flakes of fish, add the hot-smoked salmon, the parsley and the halved quails' eggs, and season with pepper. Add the diced butter, and fork everything together over a gentle heat. When you are satisfied that the heat from the rice and the gentle heat on which the pan is sitting have heated the salmon and eggs through, serve.

If reheating from frozen, allow the kedgeree to thaw overnight in a larder, and put it into the oven at 350°F/180°C/Gas Mark 4. Check after 15 minutes, stir in some cream if you like, and add the halved quails' eggs. It will take about 30 minutes, but longer if the dish is covered with foil.

Roast duck with ginger, port

and green peppercorn sauce

This recipe is intended for a domestic duck, but you can substitute wild duck, of whichever type, allowing the appropriate amount per person according to its species. But I love domestic duck, with its rich fatty meat. I do not like it undercooked: I like it roasted so that the skin is crispy and the meat cooked through. Rare-cooked duck is invariably tough. This sauce is wonderful – we use it with a variety of meats. It can be made and reheated to serve with the duck.

The average duck weighs 3–4 lb/1.35–1.7 kg and will feed 4 people, quartered. If this seems a lot given its raw weight, believe me, it isn't: a duck, like a goose, has a broad, shallow breastbone, and therefore no depth of carving whatever. To serve 6, you will have to cook 2 ducks, so 2 pieces will be left over. But cold roast duck is delicious with salad and chutney. To cut the duck easily you need a good pair of game shears or scissors.

Serves 6

2 x 3–4 lb/1.35–1.8 kg ducks
2 tsp sea salt

2 tbsp granulated sugar
¼ pint/150 ml red wine vinegar
½ pint/300 ml chicken or vegetable stock
½ pint/300 ml port
2 in/5 cm root ginger, skinned and very finely chopped
2 cloves garlic, skinned and very finely chopped
6 oz/175 g butter, diced
3 tsp green peppercorns, well drained

for the ginger, port and green peppercorn sauce

Preheat the oven to 400°F/200°C/Gas Mark 6.

Pat the ducks inside and out with a wodge of absorbent kitchen paper. Line a roasting tin with a sheet of baking parchment and put the ducks on this. Stab them with a sharp knife in several places, and scatter 1 teaspoon of salt over each. Roast for 1½–1¾ hours.

To make the sauce, put the sugar and the vinegar into a saucepan over a moderate heat and shake the pan gently until the sugar has dissolved. Then let it boil fast until the vinegar has almost evaporated and you are left with a molten caramel. Pour in the stock and the port – there will be a whoosh of steam, so beware – and add the ginger and garlic. Let the caramel melt as the port and stock heat, then let the sauce simmer gently, until the liquid has reduced by half. Take the pan off the heat, and add the butter, a little at a time, whisking it in well. Add the peppercorns, and keep the sauce warm until you are ready to serve it with the ducks.

I like baby spinach with this, wilted and mixed with butter or olive oil, some toasted pine nuts scattered over it. Serve it hot, or at room temperature. A dish of sugarsnap peas, stir fried in butter for 2 minutes then mixed with chopped mint, is also very good.

Roast goose

with prune, apple and lemon stuffing

The average goose weighs about 11 lb/5 kg, but don't be deceived into thinking that such a large bird will feed more than 6–8 people. It won't. The trouble lies in the anatomy of the goose: it has a broad shallow breastbone, so there is no depth of carving. But roast goose makes a perfect special-occasion main course for 6 people and cold roast goose is delicious. Goose is rich eating – you will get a basin of fat from one bird, which is far and away the best fat for frying or roasting potatoes.

The stuffing can be made 2–3 weeks in advance and frozen, but allow 36 hours for thawing. Make sure it has thawed completely before you put it into the bird.

Serves 6

1 x 11 lb/5 kg goose

2 tbsp olive oil *for the prune,*
2 onions, skinned and finely chopped *apple and*
6 oz/175 g long-grain rice – I use Basmati – cooked and cooled *lemon stuffing*
8 oz/225 g best-quality prunes, stoned and chopped
3 cooking apples, peeled, cored and chopped
zest and juice of 2 lemons
sea salt
plenty of freshly ground black pepper
½ tsp dried thyme, or a 2-in/5-cm sprig of fresh thyme, leaves only

about ¼ pint/150 ml goose fat *for the gravy*
1 onion, skinned and finely chopped
1 rounded tbsp flour
1 pint/600 ml chicken or vegetable stock
¼ pint/150 ml red wine
sea salt
freshly ground black pepper

To make the stuffing, heat the olive oil in a sauté pan and cook the onions until they are very soft and just beginning to colour. Let them cool. In a large bowl, mix together the cooked and cooled rice, the onions, prunes, apples, lemon zest and juice, salt, pepper and thyme. Either freeze it in a clearly labelled polythene bag, or leave it in a cool place until you are ready to stuff the goose.

Preheat the oven to 425°F/220°C/Gas Mark 7. Put the goose into the deepest roasting tin you have. Wipe out the inside of the bird with a wodge of kitchen paper, then pack in the stuffing. Cover the bird with a piece of baking parchment, and leave it in a cool place (preferably not the fridge unless there is really no alternative) until you are ready to roast it. If you do have to put it into the fridge, be sure to bring it to room temperature for an hour before you put it into the hot oven. To roast the goose, allow 20 minutes per lb/450 g, at 425°F/220°C/Gas Mark 7 for the first hour of cooking, then reduce the temperature to 400°F/200°C/Gas Mark 6.

You don't need a gravy or a sauce with the goose, but if you like one, this is simple but very good. You can ladle – with care – some of the hot goose fat from around the roasting bird half-way through the cooking time to have the gravy made well in advance of dinner. Reheat it to serve.

To make the gravy, pour the goose fat into a saucepan and sauté the finely chopped onion until it is soft. Stir in the flour and let it cook in the fat for a couple of minutes. Then gradually add the stock and the wine, stirring all the time until the gravy bubbles. Season with salt and pepper.

With the roast goose, I like to serve a purée of root vegetables, or just one vegetable, perhaps turnip – or swede, as it is called south of the border – well-flavoured with nutmeg, and whizzed in a food-processor with plenty of butter, salt, pepper and nutmeg. Cover this with sautéed cashew nuts to give a good contrasting texture. Or try the red cabbage on page 146. Neither vegetable accompaniment requires last-minute attention from the cook.

Seville orange and soy sauce marinated pheasant breasts

When pheasants have been in season for some weeks their abundance – even in the city – makes it imperative for the cook to use them. This is an easy marinade, which becomes the sauce. The recipe calls for pheasant breasts and you can buy them as such, but if you have whole birds, it takes just seconds to remove the breasts from the carcasses with a sharp knife. Either use the rest of the pheasant to make a good stock (so mild you can use it instead of chicken stock) or cut the meat off the legs, etc., and make it into game terrine. Allow for a bit of shrinkage as the pheasant breasts cook. If they are from hen pheasants, you may need more than one per person.

Serves 6

6 pheasant breasts
2 tbsp olive oil
2 oz/50 g butter
6 banana shallots, or 12 smaller ones, skinned and finely chopped
2 cloves garlic, skinned and finely chopped
1 tsp arrowroot, slaked with 2 tbsp cold water
sea salt
freshly ground black pepper

1 pint/600 ml fresh orange juice, to include the juice of 1 Seville orange *for the*
a good grating of nutmeg *marinade*
½ tsp cinnamon
2 tbsp honey
½ pint/300 ml red wine
3 tbsp best soy sauce – either Kikkoman's or Superior Soy
zest of 1 Seville orange

Arrange the pheasant breasts in a dish large enough to hold them and the marinade.

Make the marinade by heating half of the orange juice with the spices and honey. When the honey has melted into the juice take the pan off the heat and pour in the rest of the orange juice, with the red wine and the soy sauce. Stir in the orange zest, and pour the marinade over the pheasant breasts. Leave them to marinate for at least 24 hours.

When you are ready to cook them, lift the breasts out of the marinade and pat them dry with absorbent kitchen paper.

Heat the oil and the butter together in a sauté pan, and cook the breasts over a moderate heat for about 5 minutes or until they are cooked through. Then lay them in a warm serving dish. Add the shallots and the garlic to the sauté pan and cook, stirring, for 4–5 minutes, until the shallots are very soft. Pour in the marinade and let it bubble furiously, to reduce by about a third. Stir some of the hot sauce into the slaked arrowroot, pour this back into the saucepan, and stir until the sauce bubbles. Taste, and season with salt and pepper. Pour the sauce over the pheasant breasts in the warm serving dish, cover with a lid or some foil and keep the dish warm until you are ready to serve. It will keep warm without spoiling for up to 30 minutes.

I like to serve creamily mashed potatoes with this dish, and the braised red cabbage on page 146.

Tartiflette

You can prepare this dish in entirety several hours before you cook it.   **Serves 6**

2 lb/900 g floury potatoes, weighed when peeled
3 onions, skinned and sliced thinly
2 tbsp olive oil
1 whole Tomme cheese, or Reblochon, if you prefer
8 oz/225 g best ham, either roast or boiled
a grating of nutmeg
plenty of black pepper
a pinch of salt
1 pint/600 ml single cream

Preheat the oven to 350°F/180°C/Gas Mark 4.

Parboil the peeled potatoes, drain and slice them. Sauté the onions in the olive oil until they are soft, 5–7 minutes. Cut the rind off the cheese and slice it as thinly as you can. Slice the ham into neat thin strips. Butter an ovenproof dish thoroughly. Arrange in the dish a layer each of potatoes, ham, onions, and, finally, cheese. Put the cheese as the top layer, season with nutmeg, pepper and salt, then pour the cream over the top. I season first as the cream helps to distribute the flavours throughout the dish. Bake for 15 minutes, then lower the heat to 300°F/150°C/Gas Mark 2, and continue to cook until the cheese on top is melted and when you stick the point of a knife through the middle the contents feel quite soft – about 25 minutes.

The tartiflette keeps warm without deteriorating in taste or texture for a further 20 minutes or so in a very cool oven.

Ham, boiled and roast,

with shallot, red wine and orange sauce

Ham is a marvellous meat, providing that you buy the best, and for me that means organic. Ham is my only exception to my rule that I only cook meat or poultry on the bone. Off the bone, ham is much easier to handle and carve. It is so versatile: we always have hot ham, cooked to this recipe, when all the family come home at Christmas, for the first dinner when we are all together. Then we eat it cold, with buttery scrambled eggs for breakfast or lunch, and with cold turkey for supper on Boxing Night. I particularly like this sauce to go with it. And the ham stock is marvellous for split pea or lentil soup.

Serves 6

about 10 lb/4.5 kg piece of ham
1 head celery, washed and chopped in half
4 onions, halved, skin and all
a small handful of black peppercorns
4 bay leaves

for roasting **several cloves**
4 tbsp best grainy mustard, not too vinegary
3 tbsp thick honey

Put the ham into a very large saucepan and cover it with water. Add the celery, onions, peppercorns and bay leaves, and bring the water to simmering point. Cover the pan with its lid, and simmer for 15 minutes per lb/450 g. Cool the ham in the stock.

Preheat the oven to 400°F/200°C/Gas Mark 6.

Take the ham out of the stock and cut off the skin. Lay a sheet of foil in a large roasting tin, and cover it with a sheet of baking parchment. Put the skinned ham on this. Score it across with a sharp knife, cutting right through the fat. Cut it diagonally across the other way, to give you large diamond shapes. Stick a clove into each diamond. Mix together the mustard and honey, and smear it over the ham fat. Roast for 20 minutes, then lower the heat to 350°F/180°C/Gas Mark 4 and continue to roast for a further

25–30 minutes. Baste the ham with the mustard and honey mixture – which will slip off it and into the roasting tin – a couple of times. Let the ham stand out of the oven for 10 minutes before carving. Along with the shallot sauce, I like to serve roast root vegetables with the ham, and steamed leeks in white sauce. Leeks in a creamy white sauce freeze very well; thaw them overnight before reheating in a moderately hot oven.

shallot, red wine and orange sauce

Serves 6

6 banana shallots, or 12 smaller ones, skinned and finely chopped
½ pint/300 ml strained ham stock
1 pint/600 ml good red wine
juice and finely grated rind of 2 oranges
1 rounded tsp plain flour
2 oz/50 g softened butter
1 tsp redcurrant jelly
sea salt
freshly ground black pepper

Put the chopped shallots into a saucepan with the stock and red wine and simmer gently until the liquid has reduced by half. Don't be tempted to fast-boil this sauce: gently simmer it. Add the orange juice and rind. Work the flour into the butter and whisk this in, with the redcurrant jelly, until the sauce reaches simmering point once more. Simmer for a couple of minutes, taste and season with salt and pepper.

Marinated marmalade-glazed pork sausages

with onion marmalade, and butter-steamed Savoy cabbage

The longer you can marinate the sausages the better. Overnight is the minimum, but over 2 nights is better. Use the best sausages only – I reckon I'm a snob about only two things: pork sausages and ice cream! The onion marmalade is a most delicious accompaniment to the sausages and other types of grilled or baked fish and poultry. It reheats well, and can be made 3–4 days in advance.

Serves 6

2 tbsp marmalade
½ pint/300 ml good dark soy sauce – Kikkoman's is the best, and easy to buy
2 fat cloves garlic, skinned and finely chopped
pinch of powdered cinnamon
18 best pork sausages, stabbed thoroughly with a fork
2 tbsp jellied marmalade, for glazing

for the onion marmalade

5 tbsp extra-virgin olive oil
8 onions, skinned and very thinly sliced
3 tsp Demerara sugar
¼ pint/150 ml white wine vinegar
salt
freshly ground black pepper

for the butter-steamed Savoy cabbage

3 oz/75 g butter
sea salt
plenty of freshly ground black pepper
1 large or 2 smaller Savoy cabbages, trimmed of outer leaves and thinly sliced

To make the marinade, heat your chosen marmalade until it is runny, and mix it with the soy sauce, the garlic and the cinnamon in a flat dish large enough to take the sausages. Lay the sausages in the dish, coating them well with the marinade. Cover and leave them for 24–48 hours, turning them from time to time.

To make the onion marmalade, heat the oil in a large heavy-based sauté pan and put in the onions. It will look like a vast amount, but the onions will wilt as they cook. Gently sauté them, stirring occasionally, until they become very soft and reduced, about 30–35 minutes. Then stir in the Demerara sugar and let it dissolve and begin to caramelize among the onions. Add the wine vinegar, season with salt and pepper, and continue to cook, over a very low heat, for a further 20 minutes. Stir the mixture from time to time to prevent it sticking. To store, put into an airtight container and keep in the fridge.

When you are ready to cook the sausages, lift them from their marinade and drain them on 2–3 thicknesses of kitchen paper. Put them on a baking tray lined with baking parchment (this makes washing-up so much easier). Heat the jellied marmalade and brush each sausage with it before cooking them under a hot grill. Turn the sausages from time to time so that they grill evenly. When cooked, cool them a little, wrap them in greaseproof paper or a fresh sheet of baking parchment, and wrap the whole in foil to keep warm until ready to serve. They are stickily delicious.

For the cabbage, melt the butter in a large pan or ovenproof casserole, and season with salt and pepper. Put in the sliced cabbage and stir well to coat it with the seasoned butter. Clamp the lid on the pan, and either continue to cook it over a gentle heat – check occasionally that it isn't singeing on the bottom of the pan – or cover and bake it at 350°F/180°C/Gas Mark 4, for 15 minutes – a little longer if you like the cabbage more tender.

Roast loin of pork

with roast apples, shallots and juniper

Too often pork is relegated to third place in the estimation of far too many people, with beef and lamb coming first and second. Free-range pork, preferably organic, is a wonderful meat, whatever the cut, and a loin has delicious fat on top, and skin that will turn into crisp crackling. Eaten cold, roast pork is one of the best of all meats.

The roast shallots and apples around the meat benefit from being cooked in the pork fat, and the juniper enhances their flavours and that of the pork. I use a grainy mustard glaze for the pork meat, and prefer to roast the crackling separately.

Serves 6

1 x 6 lb/2.7 kg piece loin of pork, on the bone
1 tsp sea salt
2 tbsp grainy mustard
1 tbsp thick honey
6 banana shallots, skinned and halved, or 12 smaller ones, skinned and left whole
6 eating apples, peeled, cored and quartered
about 24 juniper berries, crushed

Preheat the oven to 420°F/225°C/Gas Mark 7.

If the butcher hasn't done it for you, cut the skin off the pork loin with a sharp knife. Line a roasting tin with a sheet of baking parchment, put the pork skin on the paper, scatter over it 1 teaspoon sea salt, and roast it for 40–45 minutes until it is very crisp – when you tap it, it should shatter. It will keep warm perfectly well in the bottom of the oven, so roast the crackling before you roast the meat. Lower the temperature to 400°F/200°C/Gas Mark 6.

Mix together the grainy mustard and honey, and smear this evenly over the fat on the loin. Line a roasting tin with a sheet of baking parchment, put the pork on to this and roast, allowing 20 minutes per lb/450 g. When your meat has been in the oven for 1 hour, add the shallots, apples and juniper to the tin. Stir them around a bit, so that they are covered with the fat. While the meat roasts, keep an eye on it to make sure that it isn't scorching. If it looks a bit too brown on top, lay a piece of baking parchment over it. Once the cooking time is up, leave the meat to stand for 10 minutes – this lets the juices settle. Then, on a large board, cut out the bones. This is simple to do and makes slicing the pork much easier.

To serve, slice the pork, spoon some of the apples and shallots beside it, and, if you like, serve with Vermouth gravy.

vermouth gravy

¼ pint/150 ml fat from the roasting tin
2 tsp granulated sugar
1 rounded tbsp plain flour
1 pint/600 ml vegetable stock
¼ pint/150 ml dry vermouth
sea salt
freshly ground black pepper

Put the fat into a saucepan, add the sugar and let it dissolve over a moderate heat. Let it bubble away for 2–3 minutes, until the sugar caramelizes and starts to colour the fat. Then stir in the flour, and cook for a minute before gradually pouring in the stock, stirring all the time. When the gravy reaches a gentle simmering point, cook for a minute, then stir in the vermouth. Bring it back to simmering point for a few seconds longer, take the pan off the heat, taste and season with salt and pepper.

I love cabbage with pork, and butter-steamed Savoy (see page 220) is particularly good with this. Baked sliced potatoes and onions go well, too.

Braised pork with mushrooms, garlic and red wine

We should use cuts of meat such as pork shoulder much more than we do: they need longer cooking but, providing they come from organically raised pigs, the flavour is special. As with all stews and casseroles, this one tastes even better when cooked a day in advance and reheated well before serving. It will probably need about 45 minutes in the oven if you put it in straight from the fridge, and needs only a salad and, perhaps, baked jacket potatoes to go with it.

Serves 6

2 tbsp flour

1 tsp sea salt

a good grinding of black pepper

2 lb/900 g pork shoulder, weighed when trimmed, cut into 2-in/5-cm chunks

4 tbsp olive oil

3 red onions, skinned and thinly sliced

1–2 cloves garlic, skinned and finely chopped

1½ lb/700 g mushrooms, wiped and chopped – either ordinary mushrooms
   or a mixture of wild, or dried, reconstituted wild

1 pint/600 ml red wine

1 pint/600 ml vegetable or chicken stock

Preheat the oven to 350°F/180°C/Gas Mark 4.

Mix together the flour, salt and pepper and put it into a large polythene bag with the cut-up pork. Shake the bag, to coat each bit of meat. Heat the oil in a large casserole and sear the meat a small amount at a time, so that it browns on all sides. Remove it to a warm dish. Lower the heat a little and sauté the onions until they are soft and beginning to caramelize. Add the chopped garlic when the onions are half cooked. Scoop the onion and garlic mixture from the casserole into the dish with the meat. Sauté the chopped mushrooms – you may need to add more oil to the casserole – and, as with the meat, do this in batches, to prevent the mushrooms stewing rather than sautéing. As they cook, scoop them, too, into the dish with the meat and onions. When all the mushrooms are well

winter main courses

sautéed, pour the wine and stock into the casserole, scraping the bottom to mix any meaty, mushroom or onion bits into the sauce. Stir until the liquid boils. Replace the pork, onions and mushrooms in the casserole, and stir well. Bring the liquid back to a gentle simmer, cover with a lid, and put it into the oven for 1½ hours, then reduce the temperature to 250°F/125°C/Gas Mark ½ and continue to cook for a further hour. Cool, and reheat to serve as described in the introduction.

Winter navarin of lamb

Serves 6

You can ring the changes with this extremely good winter stew by varying the root vegetables in its ingredients. You will need a large casserole with a lid, to cook it in. It doesn't freeze well once you have added the potato.

3 tbsp flour

1 tsp sea salt

½ tsp black pepper

3 lb/1.35 kg boned leg of lamb, weighed when trimmed,
   cut into 1¾-in/4.5-cm chunks

about 6 tbsp olive oil

1 tsp granulated sugar

8 banana shallots, skinned and halved lengthways or
   16 smaller ones, skinned and left whole

2 carrots

2 parsnips } peeled and cut into similar-size chunks

1 celeriac

½ turnip (swede)

2 cloves garlic, skinned and finely chopped

3 tbsp tomato purée

2 pints/1.2 litres beef or vegetable stock

2 bay leaves

1 sprig thyme, 3 in/7.5 cm long

1½ lb/700 g potatoes, weighed when peeled, cut into 1-in/2.5-cm chunks

Put the flour, salt and pepper into a large polythene bag and toss the trimmed lamb in this, until each piece of meat is coated with seasoned flour. Heat the olive oil in a large casserole and brown the meat in relays, sprinkling in a little granulated sugar with each batch – this helps both the colour and taste of the finished Navarin. As the meat is browned, remove it to a warmed dish. Then, adding a little more oil to the casserole if needed, sauté the shallots on a moderate heat until they are turning golden. Add the rest of the vegetables, with the garlic, stir them well in the oil, and cook for a few minutes.

winter main courses

Meanwhile, mix the tomato purée into the stock. Pour it into the casserole, then stir and scrape the base until the liquid simmers gently. Add the bay leaves and thyme, and replace the meat among the vegetables. Bring the liquid back to a simmer, cover with a lid, and put the casserole into the oven for 1 hour. Take it out, let it cool, and store it in a cold place.

To reheat, add the potatoes to the casserole, reheat until the liquid is simmering, then cover with the lid once more, and put it into the oven at 350°F/180°C/Gas Mark 4 for a further 45 minutes. Test a piece of potato to see if it is tender by pushing a knife into a chunk. Remove the bay leaves and thyme if you can find them, and serve.

This will keep warm without spoiling for up to 1 hour.

Oxtail and root vegetable stew

There is no better stew than one made with oxtail. I felt positively deprived while beef-on-the-bone was banned. I can live without T-bone steaks but oxtail is a different matter! Oxtail stew freezes well, although oxtail is the one cut of meat that does not freeze successfully raw. The sweetness of root vegetables is perfect with the richness of the meat. It is virtually impossible to overcook oxtail – it should be dropping off the bones. Those of us lucky enough to own an Aga or a Raeburn have the perfect and economical method of cooking such a stew as this. As with any stew or casserole, this benefits from being made a day in advance and reheated to serve.

Serves 6

4 tbsp olive oil
2 oxtails, as much fat trimmed off as possible
2 onions, skinned and sliced or neatly chopped
2 fat cloves garlic, skinned and chopped
3 leeks, trimmed, washed and sliced
2 parsnips, peeled and neatly chopped
1 lb/450 g Jerusalem artichokes, peeled and the larger ones cut in half
1 tbsp flour
about 2 tbsp tomato purée
1 pint/600 ml water
1 pint/600 ml lager
sea salt
freshly ground black pepper

Preheat the oven to 250°F/120°C/Gas Mark ½.

Heat the oil in a large, heavy casserole and brown the pieces of oxtail all over. As they brown – and this takes some time – remove them to a warm dish. When all the pieces of oxtail are browned, lower the heat and add the onions to the casserole. Cook them for 7–10 minutes, stirring occasionally. Then put in the garlic and leeks and cook for about 5 minutes – they need less time to brown than the onions. Scoop out the onions and leeks and add the parsnips and artichokes. Stir them around and sauté them for 5–7 minutes. Scatter in the flour, stir it in well, and let it cook for a minute before adding the tomato purée. Stir in the water and lager and keep stirring until the liquid bubbles among the vegetables. Season with salt and pepper, stir again, then replace the leeks and onions, and lastly the pieces of oxtail, pushing them down among the rest of the contents of the casserole. Put on the lid, bring the liquid back to bubbling point, then put the casserole into the oven for 3–3½ hours. Take it out and leave it to cool completely, overnight in a cold place – ideally a larder, or the fridge.

To reheat, I bring the thickened liquid up to simmering point on the hob, replace the lid then put the casserole back into the oven at 250°F/120°C/Gas Mark ½ for at least 2 hours. Longer won't hurt it a bit.

This is delicious with well-mashed or baked jacket potatoes, and, if you like, cabbage or Brussels sprouts.

Venison pudding

with lemon suet crust

Venison is such a good red meat, rich in flavour and lean. This slow-cooked pudding is a tasty and comforting winter dish. Convenient, too, because it can be made a day or two in advance and steamed again to reheat for serving, which actually improves the flavours. Those plastic snap-lid pudding bowls, which are impervious to boiling water, are a real boon for those who, like me, can't tie a tight enough knot to secure a muslin covering for a steamed pudding. Don't forget to check the water level in the saucepan around the pudding while it cooks. Tragedy is the result when you let a steamed pudding boil dry. It is the sort of event that occurs only once in your life, and when I did it, I lost the pudding, the saucepan and the plastic bowl, which melted into the pan!

Serves 6

for the suet pastry
12 oz/350 g self-raising flour, sieved
6 oz/175 g shredded suet
zest of 2 lemons
sea salt
freshly ground black pepper

for the filling
2 lb/900 g venison, weighed when trimmed of sinew or membrane,
**   cut into 1-in/2.5-cm chunks**
1 onion, skinned and finely chopped
2 tbsp flour
½ tsp sea salt
freshly ground black pepper
½ pint/300 ml hot water
2 tsp redcurrant jelly
½ pint/300 ml red wine

Mix together the pastry ingredients and bind them together with cold water to a dough. Roll out ⅔ of the dough, and use it to line a 4-pint/2.2-litre pudding bowl.

In a large bowl, mix together the chunks of venison, the onion, flour, salt and pepper. Pack this into the pastry-lined bowl. Warm the water and dissolve the redcurrant jelly in it. Mix this with the red wine, and pour it around the venison. Roll out the remaining third of the dough, and use it to cover the pudding, crimping together the edges. Cover with a disc of baking parchment, and snap on the lid if you are using a plastic bowl that can be boiled. Otherwise, seal the bowl with a layer of foil, and tie a muslin cloth securely over the pudding. Put the pudding into a large saucepan, and pour boiling water half-way up the sides of the bowl. Cover the pan with its lid, and heat it until the water reaches boiling point once more, then simmer for 5 hours if you are going to serve the pudding straight away, or for 3½–4 hours if you intend to reheat it to serve the next day. If you make the pudding in advance, steam it for a further 2–2½ hours before serving.

Do be careful when you are lifting the bowl out of the pan: I will never forget the agony when I dropped a steak and kidney pud on my foot just after lifting it out of the pan. I hopped around in exquisite agony while the family were vastly relieved to discover that the pudding was still intact!

Serve with butter-steamed Savoy cabbage (see page 220) or perhaps roast parsnips, which go very well with venison pudding.

Sliced clementines in caramel

with caramel cream

Clementines are the smell and taste of Christmas, but they do vary in quality – like most fruits brought into this country. However, no clementine is ever as dreary as a satsuma, with its watery flesh and baggy skin. This simple pudding makes the most of these seasonal fruits.

Serves 6

12 clementines

for the caramel   **6 oz/175 g granulated sugar**

for the caramel cream   **4 oz/110 g granulated sugar**
6 tbsp either water or lemon juice and water mixed
½ pint/300 ml double cream

With a sharp serrated knife cut the skin and pith from the fruit. Then slice each clementine as thinly as possible, carefully removing any pips. Arrange them in a shallow serving dish, or alternatively stack up the slices to reform the shape of the fruit.

In a heavy-bottomed saucepan dissolve the 6 oz/175 g granulated sugar over a gentle heat. Don't try to hurry this, because if the sugar burns you have no alternative but to start again. Once the sugar starts to dissolve, it is a fairly fast process. Shake the pan through-out, never stir. When you have a golden molten caramel, pour this over the sliced or stacked clementines. Most of the crisp caramel will dissolve in the juice.

To make the cream, repeat the caramelizing process with the 4 oz/110 g sugar. When the sugar is molten, take the pan off the heat for a minute before you add the lemon juice and water. There will be a whoosh of steam. Over gentle heat, dissolve the caramel in the liquid, taking care not to let it burn in the process. When you have a smooth syrup, take the pan off the heat, and let it cool.

Whip the double cream to soft peaks, then gradually whip in the cold caramel syrup.

Pink grapefruit and Campari jellied terrine

with pink grapefruit and orange compote with caramelized peel

*For those who, like me, love Campari this is a deliciously fresh way to finish
a rich lunch or dinner. If you prefer, use fresh orange juice instead of the pink
grapefruit juice. If you set the jelly in a metal loaf tin, line it first with clingfilm. Use a 2-lb/900-g loaf tin or a terrine-shaped Pyrex dish.*   **Serves 6**

2 sachets powdered gelatine or 8 leaves sheet gelatine
1½ pints/900 ml pink grapefruit juice
2 pink grapefruit
2 oz/50 g caster sugar
¼ pint/150 ml Campari

4 more pink grapefruit   *for the compote*
4 oranges
6 oz/175 g granulated sugar
½ pint/300 ml grapefruit and orange juices collected
from the preparation of the segments

If you are using leaf gelatine, soak the leaves in a little cold water
for several minutes. If you are using powdered gelatine, measure
½ pint/300 ml of the grapefruit juice into a saucepan and sprinkle in
the gelatine. Let it become spongy in the liquid, then, over a gentle
heat, shake the pan until every granule of gelatine has dissolved. If
you are using leaf gelatine heat ½ pint/300 ml of the grapefruit juice
in a saucepan and when the liquid is very hot, but not boiling, lift the
soaked jelly-like leaves into the hot liquid where they will melt almost
instantly.

With a serrated knife cut the skin and pith from the 2 grapefruit
and, slicing between the membranes, cut into the centre of each
fruit and remove the segments. Arrange these on the base of the
loaf tin.

Stir the caster sugar into the hot gelatine liquid, stirring until it has
dissolved. Pour this into a jug or bowl with the rest of the pink grapefruit juice, and stir in the Campari. Pour it into the tin over the

segments, just to cover them, and put the terrine into the fridge to set. Meanwhile, keep the rest of the pink grapefruit and Campari liquid just warm so that it doesn't set. When the segments are set in their jelly, pour in the rest of the liquid, and put it back into the fridge to set again.

For the compote, wash all the fruit thoroughly. With a potato peeler, pare the rind from 2 grapefruit and 2 oranges. Then, with a sharp knife, cut the rind into thin strips. Put them into a saucepan, cover them with cold water to a depth of several inches and simmer for 20 minutes. Then drain them. Put into the saucepan the sugar and the ½ pint/300 ml of juice – if there isn't quite enough make it up with water. Shake the pan over a moderate heat and stir until the sugar has dissolved, then boil fast for 3–5 minutes. Add the strips of peel, and simmer in the syrup for 3–5 minutes. Meanwhile, with a serrated knife, cut the skin and pith from the remaining pink grape-fruit and oranges, and cut into the centre of the fruits to extract the segments minus their membranes. Put the fruit into a serving bowl, and mix in the strips of caramelized peel and any remaining syrup, stirring well.

To serve, dip the terrine containing the jelly briefly in hot water and invert it over a serving plate. Peel off the clingfilm. Slice the terrine and put a piece with a small spoonful of compote on each plate.

Baked blueberry, lemon and almond pudding

All the tastes I love are combined in this pudding. It's delicious!   **Serves 6**

**2 lb/900 g blueberries, or frozen brambles, or apples
(peeled, cored and chopped) or sliced plums, weighed after stoning
3–6 oz/75–150 g sugar, or to taste
zest of 1 lemon**

4 oz/110 g self-raising flour   *for the*
2 oz/50 g ground almonds, dry-fried to toast them   *pudding mixture*
**3 oz/75 g caster sugar
3 oz/75 g butter, melted and cooled
1 large egg
¼ pint/150 ml buttermilk or whole milk
zest of 1 lemon
a few drops of almond extract
2 tbsp flaked almonds**

Preheat the oven to 350°F/180°C/Gas Mark 4.

Butter a 9 x 12-in/23 x 30-cm ovenproof dish. Put the blueberries into the dish. Mix in the sugar and lemon zest.

Make the pudding mixture: sieve the flour into a bowl. Add the cooled ground almonds and the sugar. Beat in the melted butter, the egg, buttermilk, lemon zest and almond extract. Spoon this over the fruit, leaving about 1 in/2.5 cm of fruit uncovered around the sides. Sprinkle the flaked almonds over the top and bake until the fruit is bubbling and the pudding is browned, about 40 minutes.

Serve with *crème fraîche* or vanilla ice cream, or with a vanilla-and-lemon-flavoured custard.

Baked spiced apricot fudge pudding

The best apricots for this recipe are the semi-dried ones. If you use ordinary dried apricots, simmer them gently in water first with the juice of half a lemon. Drain them well, before making the fudge sauce. When this pudding is turned out the apricots in the fudgey goo are uppermost. If you don't like ginger, leave it out. This pudding freezes and reheats well.

Serves 6

4 oz/110 g butter

8 oz/225 g soft brown sugar

8 oz/225 g semi-dried apricots

6 pieces preserved ginger, drained and chopped, optional

*for the
pudding mixture*

8 oz/225 g self-raising flour

1 level tsp bicarbonate of soda

2 tsp ground cinnamon

½ nutmeg, grated

2 tsp ground ginger

zest and juice of 2 lemons

zest and juice of 2 oranges

6 fl oz/175 ml milk

2 large eggs, beaten

8 oz/225 g soft brown sugar

6 tbsp black treacle

4 oz/110 g melted butter

Preheat the oven to 350°F/180°C/Gas Mark 4.

Put the butter and sugar together into a saucepan over moderate heat and let them dissolve together – don't let the mixture boil before the sugar has dissolved. Then bubble it gently, stirring, for 2 minutes. Pour it into a shallow 3-pint/1.7-litre ovenproof dish. Arrange the apricots and chopped ginger over the fudge.

Make the pudding mixture by sieving together the flour, bicarbonate of soda, cinnamon, nutmeg and ginger into a bowl. Add the lemon and orange zests. In another bowl, mix together the milk, eggs, sugar, treacle and melted butter. Beat this into the dry ingredients, add the lemon and orange juice, and mix thoroughly. Pour and scrape this over the apricots and fudge. Bake for 40–45 minutes, or until firm to the touch.

Serve warm. I like it with *crème fraîche*, but a warm vanilla custard is also very good. Or both.

Baked orange and lemon pudding

with spiced cranberries

Cranberries are a wonderful winter fruit. We can buy them fresh even as far north as Skye. They keep well, freeze well, and are excellent combined with citrus and spices. This pudding can be made in advance and reheated to serve. I have frozen, thawed and reheated it without any apparent deterioration in either texture or flavour.

Serves 6

1 lb/450 g cranberries
juice of 2 oranges
1 cinnamon stick
about ½ tsp freshly grated nutmeg
3 oz/75 g soft dark brown sugar

for the pudding

4 oz/110 g butter
8 oz/225 g caster sugar
5 large eggs, separated
zest and juice of 2 lemons
zest of 1 orange
2 oz/50 g plain flour, sieved
½ pint/300 ml milk

Preheat the oven to 350°F/180°C/Gas Mark 4.

Put the cranberries and the orange juice into a saucepan and cook gently until the berries are soft. Then add the cinnamon stick, the nutmeg, and the soft brown sugar. Stir until the sugar has dissolved, then continue to cook for a couple of minutes. Take the pan off the heat and let the fruit cool. When it is cold, remove the cinnamon stick and pour the fruit and its juices into a 4-pint/2.2-litre ovenproof dish.

To make the pudding mixture, cream together the butter and sugar until the mixture is pale and fluffy. Beat in the egg yolks, one by one – don't worry if the mixture curdles, it won't affect the end result. Beat in the lemon and orange zest, the lemon juice, the flour and, lastly, the milk. The batter will be fairly sloppy.

winter puddings

In a clean bowl, whisk the egg whites until they are very stiff and, with a large metal spoon, fold them quickly and thoroughly through the pudding mixture, making sure that there are no little pockets of egg white. Pour this over the cooked cranberries, put the pudding into a roasting tin with boiling water poured in to come half-way up the sides of the dish. Carefully put the roasting tin and its contents into the oven and bake for 40–45 minutes, until the pudding feels quite firm when you press the top. If it begins to turn brown early in the cooking time, put a sheet of baking parchment on top.

This pud keeps warm almost endlessly. If you make it on the day when it is to be served, you can forget about it in a very low oven for up to 2 hours. Serve it with either whipped cream or *crème fraîche*.

Baked lemon cream rice pudding

Rice pudding was the one thing we ate at my boarding-school that was not only edible but delicious. But this rice pudding is a far cry even from that. It is such a convenient pud, too, because it just sits in a low oven for ages without spoiling. And it takes only minutes to put together.

Serves 6

3 oz/75 g round-grain pudding rice
1 pint/600 ml full-fat milk
½ tsp vanilla extract, or 1 vanilla pod, split
6 tbsp maple syrup or 4 oz/110 g soft brown sugar
zest of 1½ lemons
½ pint/300 ml double cream

Preheat the oven to 275°F/140°C/Gas Mark 1, and butter a 3-pint/1.7-litre ovenproof dish.

Put the rice and milk into a saucepan and heat until the milk is simmering around the rice. Cook gently for 5 minutes, stirring. Take the saucepan off the heat and add the split vanilla pod or the vanilla extract, the maple syrup, lemon zest and the cream. Mix well, and pour it into the buttered dish. Bake for 2 hours. Lower the temperature further if you want to keep the pudding warm before serving. It will make for a most delicious skin on the surface. To serve, remove the vanilla pod and spoon it into bowls.

Panettone and apricot Marsala trifle

Panettone varies so much, but for this I like to use a standard one, not chocolate but a vanilla-scented panettone with mixed dried fruit, thinly sliced and spread with the best apricot jam I can buy. The flavour of the Marsala in the creamy custard is particularly good with the apricot jam and the panettone. This trifle is better made several hours ahead, or even left overnight in the fridge; just finish it off with the cream and chocolate on the day you plan to eat it.

Serves 6

1 pint/600 ml single cream   *for the custard*
6 large egg yolks
3 oz/75 g caster sugar
4 tbsp Marsala

1 small panettone, thinly sliced
1 x 1lb/450 g jar best apricot jam

½ pint/300 ml double cream, whipped   *to finish*
3 oz/75 g dark chocolate, coarsely grated   *the trifle*

Start by making the Marsala custard. Put the cream into a saucepan over a moderate heat until it is steaming – be careful not to let it boil. Meanwhile, beat together the egg yolks and the caster sugar, then stir in the cream. Cook the custard either by putting the bowl over a saucepan of simmering water and stirring until the custard thickens, which takes about 30 minutes, or, if you have a microwave oven, cook it in that. Put in the bowl of custard on high for 1 minute, take it out, whisk the contents well, then replace it in the microwave oven for 30 seconds on medium. Whisk the contents and repeat until the custard is thick enough to coat the back of your wooden spoon. When the custard has thickened, stir in the Marsala. Leave it to cool.

Spread each slice of panettone with apricot jam and lay some over the base of a serving dish. Pour in a little of the Marsala custard, just enough to coat the panettone. Cover with the rest of the panettone, then pour over the rest of the custard.

To finish, cover with whipped cream, and shavings of dark chocolate: hold the chocolate in a double thickness of foil to prevent it melting, and shave it with a potato-peeler.

Vanilla panna cotta

with Seville orange compote

Literally translated this is 'cooked cream'. It should be barely set and it is delicious with any sharp fruit or fruity sauce, such as bitter orange and lemon, or, in season, raspberries or blackcurrants.

Serves 4

1 pint/600 ml single cream *for the*
2 oz/50 g caster sugar *panna cotta*
1 vanilla pod or a few drops vanilla extract
1 leaf gelatine, or 1 tsp powdered gelatine

2 Seville oranges *for the compote*
1 lemon
1 pint/600 ml water
3 oz/75 g granulated sugar

To make the panna cotta, put the cream, sugar and split vanilla pod into a saucepan over a moderate heat. Stir until the sugar has dissolved and the cream is scalding but not boiling. Take the cream off the heat and leave it to cool, then lift out the vanilla pod. Scrape it well so that the tiny seeds fall into the cream. Then wash the pod, if it is a fresh one, and store it to use once more.

Soak the gelatine leaf in a little water for a few minutes, and mix this into the cream. Heat gently, stirring, until it has melted. If you are using powdered gelatine, soak it in 2 teaspoons of cold water before you stir it into the cream. If you are using vanilla extract instead of a vanilla pod, add a few drops to the cream.

Strain the cream, and divide it between 4 glasses. Leave it to set.

To make the compote, slice the oranges and lemon thinly, then quarter each slice. Put them with the water into a saucepan and simmer over a moderate heat, with the pan uncovered, until the thickest piece of peel feels quite soft when you push a fork into it. The liquid should have reduced by about half. Then add the sugar and stir until it has dissolved. Let the liquid return to the boil, then turn down the heat and simmer gently for 3–5 minutes.

To serve, spoon the compote over the panna cotta in the glasses.

Vanilla meringue

with dark chocolate cream and marrons glacés

*This is my favourite of all puddings, its combination of tastes and textures –
but I wouldn't make it in summer: this simple but special meringue cake is
the essence of Christmas and New Year. The vanilla meringues can be made
up to 10 days in advance, providing you store them in an airtight container.
Buy two extra marrons, and eat them as you assemble the pudding – you
deserve them! It is easier to cut if you put it together several hours before
you plan to eat it and keep it in the fridge.*

Serves 6

3 large egg whites
a pinch of salt
6 oz/175 g caster sugar
a few drops vanilla extract *or* ½ tsp vanilla essence

for the filling

½ pint/300 ml double cream, whipped
6 oz/175 g dark chocolate
6 marrons glacés, cut into slivers

To make the meringues, line two 9-in/23-cm cake tins with discs of
baking parchment. Preheat the oven to 250°F/125°C/Gas Mark ½. In
a bowl whisk the egg whites with the salt until they are stiff. Then
add the sugar, a spoonful at a time, whisking continuously to a stiff
meringue. Lastly whisk in the vanilla.

Divide the meringue between the prepared cake tins, smoothing
the mixture to within 1–1½ in/2.5 cm of the edge of the paper. Bake
for 2–2½ hours. Let the cooked meringues cool on a wire rack.
Carefully peel off the baking parchment while they are still warm –
easier than when they are cold. Store them in an airtight container.

To assemble, put a dab of whipped cream on to the serving plate,
and put one meringue on this – the cream helps to prevent the
meringue cake skidding around the plate. Grate 4 oz/110 g of the
chocolate coarsely: hold the chocolate in a double thickness of foil to
prevent it melting in your hand. Spread the cream over the meringue,
and spoon the chocolate over it, gently pressing it in. Don't be

winter puddings

tempted to fold together the whipped cream and grated chocolate: it forms such a solid mass that it is impossible to spread. Cover the chocolate cream with slivers of the marrons glacés, pressing them into the cream, too. Cover with the remaining meringue half. Shave the rest of the chocolate with a potato-peeler into shavings, and scatter them over the surface and the sides of the plate.

To serve, slice the meringue cake with a serrated knife – or, for the most professional results, with an electric carving knife.

Dark chocolate crème brûlée

with crystallized pink grapefruit peel

Serves 6

This isn't a true crème brûlée as it contains no egg yolks. It doesn't need them: as the chocolate and cream mixture gets cold, it solidifies. It is so simple, and benefits from being made, but not brûléed, a couple of days in advance. The crystallized pink grapefruit peel is utterly wonderful: I encountered it in the French Alps on holiday, came home and promptly made some myself. It goes so well with this chocolate cream, and keeps well in a covered container for several days.

for the dark chocolate brûlée

¾ pint/450 ml double cream

12 oz/350 g dark chocolate, broken into bits

scant ½ tsp powdered cinnamon

a few drops vanilla extract

2 tsp caster sugar per person, for the brûlé topping

for the crystallized pink grapefruit peel

2 pink grapefruit

1 lb/450 g granulated sugar

1 pint/600 ml water

extra granulated sugar, in which to roll the finished strips of peel

Put the cream, chocolate, cinnamon and vanilla into a saucepan over a low to moderate heat. Stir, until you have a thick, rich, dark, glossy cream. Divide it between 6 ramekins, cover, and leave for several hours or, better still, overnight – even over two nights – and the chocolate will set firmly.

Before serving, put 2 teaspoons of caster sugar on each ramekin, and shake gently so that it covers the surface evenly. Preheat the grill to red-hot, stand the ramekins on a baking sheet and put them as high under the grill as you can. Watch them like a hawk, and as soon as the sugar has melted, take them out, and leave them to cool. Alternatively, if you have a blow-torch, use that to dissolve the sugar to a caramel.

With a sharp serrated knife cut the peel from the grapefruit, and slice it into 2-in/5-cm strips about ½ in/1 cm thick. Put them into cold water and leave overnight.

winter puddings

Drain off the water, put the peel strips into a saucepan, cover them with cold water and simmer until the strips of peel look clear and are tender when you push a fork into them. Drain off the cooking water. Put the sugar and the water into a saucepan and heat gently until the sugar has dissolved. Then – and only then – boil fast for 5 minutes. Put the peel into the sugar syrup and simmer, over a moderate heat, until it has more or less absorbed all of the syrup. Dip each strip of crystallized peel into the granulated sugar, and leave them on baking parchment at room temperature for up to 24 hours. Store them in a container, with a tight-fitting lid, lined with baking parchment, and with more parchment between each layer of peel. Store in a cool place, ideally a larder.

Serve each ramekin of Dark Chocolate Crème Brûlée with 2 strips of the crystallized peel.

Instead of using it to accompany a pudding, try dipping half of each strip of crystallized peel in melted dark chocolate. Lay them to cool on baking parchment then store in an airtight container.

Dark chocolate and cinnamon ice

This ice, which has little cream in it, satisfies my passion for chocolate and at the same time is very light. I love the way the flavours of cinnamon, coffee and vanilla enhance the flavour of dark chocolate. It is important to whiz the semi-frozen ice thoroughly during the freezing process. I try to do this 3 times, and set my timer to remind me during the day I make it. Alternatively, you can freeze and churn it in an ice-cream machine if you have one.

Serves 6

3 oz/75 g best cocoa powder, Green and Black's, if possible
8 oz/225 g caster sugar
1 rounded tsp ground cinnamon
6 gratings nutmeg
½ pint/300 ml cold water
½ tsp vanilla extract or 1 tsp essence
½ pint/300 ml single cream

Put the cocoa, sugar, cinnamon and nutmeg into a saucepan and mix in the water until you have a smooth cream. Stir over a moderate heat until the sugar has dissolved, then bring it to a rolling boil, and boil for 2 minutes. Watch that it doesn't boil over. Take the pan off the heat, then stir in the vanilla and the cream. Pour into a solid container with a lid and freeze for 3 hours or so. Then scrape the contents into a food-processor and whiz. Refreeze and repeat twice at 3-hour intervals. The whizzing breaks down the ice crystals and gives you a smooth ice.

To serve, take the ice out of the freezer half an hour before you need it, and let it sit at room temperature to soften a little. It is very good with crisp ginger biscuits.

winter puddings

Iced Christmas bombe

This can, of course, be eaten as a special pudding at any time during the season when marrons glacés are available. You can make it up to a month ahead of when you want to eat it. The Warm Dark Chocolate Sauce (see page 56) would go well with it – but perhaps that would be lily-gilding. You can make the meringues up to 10 days ahead of when you will need them.

Serves 6 generously

6 large egg whites
pinch of salt
6 oz/175 g caster sugar
a very few drops vanilla extract
3 oz/75 g best raisins, Lexia, or semi-dried grapes
5 fl oz/150 ml brandy or freshly squeezed orange juice
3 oz/75 g icing sugar, sieved
½ pint/300 ml double cream
4 oz/110 g best dark chocolate, coarsely grated
6 marrons glacés, chopped

Start by making the meringues. Preheat the oven to 225°F/110°C/Gas Mark ¼. Whisk 3 of the egg whites in a bowl with a pinch of salt until stiff. Then, whisking all the time, gradually add the caster sugar, a spoonful at a time, and keep whisking until all is incorporated and you have a stiff meringue. Lastly, whisk in the vanilla extract. Line a baking tray with a sheet of baking parchment then spoon on even-sized dollops of meringue and bake for 2½ hours. When cooked the meringues should lift off the paper easily. Cool them, and store them in an airtight container.

Marinate the raisins in the brandy or orange juice overnight in a covered bowl.

For the ice cream, whisk the remaining whites with a pinch of salt until they are stiff. Then gradually whisk in the icing sugar a spoonful at a time, until it has all been incorporated. Then whip the cream to soft peaks.

Line a 4-pint/2.2-litre pudding bowl with clingfilm. Scrunch the meringues into the whipped cream, then fold in the grated chocolate, the plumped-up raisins and the marrons. Fold in the raw meringue mixture. Pack this into the pudding bowl, and bang it 2–3 times on the work surface to remove any air pockets. Cover the bowl and freeze.

To turn out, take the cover off the bowl. Dip the bowl briefly into a basin of very hot water, and turn out the bombe on to a serving plate. Serve it in slices, accompanied, if you like, with Warm Dark Chocolate Sauce (see page 56).

Egg nog mousse

This boozy mousse slips down a treat. Its flavours are redolent of Christmas and New Year, with the rum, nutmeg and dark chocolate. The traditional Christmas egg nog drink is more like a pudding than a drink anyway, so it seems entirely sensible to enjoy it, set, as a pud.

It can be made a day in advance, but take the mousse into room temperature for at least 30 minutes before serving.

Serves 6

5 fl oz/150 ml dark rum
1 sachet gelatine
4 large eggs, separated
6 oz/175 g caster sugar
⅓ tsp freshly grated nutmeg
½ pint/300 ml double cream, whipped
4 oz/110 g dark chocolate, shaved

Pour the rum into a small saucepan over a low heat, add the gelatine and stir until it has dissolved. Whisk the egg yolks with 4 oz/110 g of the caster sugar, until the mixture is very thick and pale. Whisk in the rum and gelatine and the nutmeg. Fold in the whipped cream. Whisk the egg whites until they are stiff, then gradually whisk in the remaining 2 oz/50 g caster sugar.

With a large metal spoon, fold the meringue into the rum mixture. Pour into a glass or china serving bowl, or into 6 glasses, and strew the shaved dark chocolate over the surface. Leave in a cool place, a larder or a fridge, to set.

Cinnamon ice cream

with baked gingerbread and black pepper pudding

The Baked Gingerbread and Black Pepper Pudding warms up well so can be made in advance. Don't be tempted to do this in the microwave though – it seems to dry out the pudding.

Serves 6

for the ice cream

3 large eggs, separated

3 oz/75 g icing sugar, sieved

2 tsp powdered cinnamon

1 pint/600 ml double cream, whipped to soft peaks

for the gingerbread pudding

4 oz/110 g self-raising flour

2 tsp ground cinnamon

1 tsp ground ginger

a pinch of ground cloves

a grating of nutmeg

½ tsp bicarbonate of soda

4 oz/110 g soft light brown sugar

1 large egg

3 oz/75 g black treacle

5 fl oz/140 ml milk

2 oz/50 g butter, melted

grated zest of 1 orange

½ tsp coarsely ground black pepper

6 pieces preserved stem ginger, drained and chopped

3 oz/75 g raisins

Whisk the egg whites until they are stiff, and then, whisking continuously, add 2 oz/50 g of the icing sugar, a teaspoon at a time. You should end up with a stiff meringue mixture. Then whisk the yolks, adding the remaining icing sugar, and the cinnamon, until they are thick. Fold the yolk mixture into the whipped cream, then the meringue. Freeze in a solid polythene container. Take the ice cream out of the freezer and put it into the fridge before dinner to allow it to soften a little before serving.

Preheat the oven to 350°F/180°C/Gas Mark 4.

Sieve the flour and the dry ingredients into a bowl, then add the egg, treacle, milk, melted butter, orange zest and black pepper. Mix thoroughly, then stir in the chopped ginger and the raisins. Pour the gingerbread mixture into a well-buttered ovenproof dish. Bake for 30–35 minutes.

Serve warm, with the cinnamon ice cream.

A winter picnic

We invariably have a picnic during December or January – perhaps two. When it is a bright day, nowhere on earth could be more beautiful than Skye, with the snow on the mountains and the blue sky. But there is no point in pretending it might be warm: we build a bonfire on the beach, and make sure the food is warming. The lentil and chilli soup isn't fiery hot, but it contains just enough chilli to give you a glow when you eat it. I like to make it with ham stock.

If I am feeding a large number of people, like the hotel guests around New Year, we take along a calor-gas-fuelled large griddle. This is ideal for cooking the chunks of marinated venison. Otherwise, for up to 6 people, an old frying-pan on the bonfire will suffice. Nothing is better than a rich fruit cake eaten with a piece of Stilton, and after that, toasted marshmallows, but I only like the white ones! Whisky Mac is the ideal drink to accompany a winter picnic.

lentil and chilli soup

Serves 6

3 tablespoons olive oil
2 onions, skinned and chopped
3 carrots, peeled and chopped into large dice
1 parsnip, peeled and diced
1–2 cloves garlic, skinned and chopped, optional
6 oz/175 g red lentils
2 pints/1.2 litres ham stock, or any other good stock
½ tsp flaked dried chilli
sea salt – if you don't use ham stock
freshly ground black pepper

Heat the oil in a large saucepan and sauté the chopped onions until they are soft and transparent. Add carrots, parsnip and garlic and cook for about 5 minutes, stirring occasionally. Then stir in the lentils, pour in the stock, and add the chilli. Bring the stock to simmering point, then half cover the pan with its lid, and cook gently for 25–30 minutes, or until the carrot is very tender.

If you have a Braun hand-blender, use it in the pan partially to blend the soup. Otherwise, put half of the soup into a blender, whiz, and stir it back into the rest in the saucepan. Taste, and season with salt, if it is needed, and black pepper. Reheat the soup, and pour it into wide-necked Thermos flasks to transport it to the picnic site.

Serve with buttered oatcakes, stuck together like sandwiches – they are delicious, with the soup and the venison chunks – or with buttered white or brown rolls.

marinated venison chunks

You need a tender cut for this, from the rump. Marinate the meat for up to 48 hours in a cool place. You will need good-quality rigid waxed paper plates to serve the venison on. If you would prefer, you can sauté the pieces of meat at home and transport them wrapped in foil rather than cooking it on the bonfire or a gas-fuelled griddle. Your bonfire can be for warmth and marshmallow toasting! Marinated Pork Sausages (see page 220) would make a perfect alternative main course.

Serves 6

3 lb/1.35 kg rump venison, cut into ½-in/1-cm chunks, trimmed of any sinew

½ pint/300 ml extra-virgin olive oil *for the*
6 tbsp strong soy sauce – the best is Superior Soy *marinade*
3 fat cloves garlic, skinned and chopped
2 oz/50 g black peppercorns, crushed
about 2 tbsp chopped parsley

Mix together all the ingredients for the marinade in a fairly wide shallow dish. Stir in the meat, coating each piece. Leave for up to 48 hours, but turn the meat in the marinade from time to time.

To cook, lift the meat from the dish, drip off any excess liquid, and sear it over a very high heat.

Delicious with buttered oatcakes and Lentil and Chilli soup.

rich fruit cake with Stilton

The longer ahead this is made the very much better the cake will be. Much as I enjoy a good fruit cake, I prefer it uncooked. When I'm making this cake any dietary thoughts fly out of the window as I lick out the mixing bowl.

Serves 6, with about half of the cake left over

10 oz/275 g plain flour, sieved
2 tsp ground ginger
½ a nutmeg, grated
2 tsp mixed spice
2 tsp ground cinnamon
8 oz/225 g sultanas
8 oz/225 g raisins
12 oz/350 g currants
4 oz/110 g chopped fresh candied peel
6–8 pieces preserved ginger, chopped
6 oz/175 g prunes, stoned and chopped
6 oz/175 g flaked almonds, dry-fried until light brown
10 oz/275 g butter
10 oz/275 g soft light brown sugar
grated zest and juice of 2 lemons and 1 orange
5 large eggs
¼ pint/150 ml whisky or brandy

Stilton, to serve with the cake

Butter a 10-in/25-cm deep cake tin thoroughly, then line it with baking parchment. Preheat the oven to 350°F/180°C/Gas Mark 4.

Put the flour into a large mixing-bowl and add the spices, dried fruits and ginger. Stir well, so that each piece of fruit is coated with the flour. Add the toasted flaked almonds. In a separate bowl cream the butter with the sugar,until the mixture is light and almost fluffy. Beat in the lemon and orange zest and juice. Beat the eggs with the whisky or brandy. Beat the butter mixture into the dry ingredients, alternating with the egg mixture, until everything is thoroughly mixed together. Put the cake mixture into the prepared tin, smooth it even, then make a hollow in the centre with the back of a wooden spoon. Bake for 30 minutes. Then reduce the oven temperature to 300°F/150°C/Gas Mark 2 and bake for 1½ hours. Push a sharp knife into the centre of the cake – it should come out clean. But I like to undercook my cake slightly, and if the knife is still sticky, I take it out of the oven anyway. Cool the cake in its tin, then, when it is cold, turn it out, wrap it in a double thickness of foil, and store it in a cool place, ideally a larder.

Either cut the cake before departing for the picnic, or remember to take a knife with you. The same applies to the Stilton. If you don't want to take the whole cheese with you, cut some slices (horizontally, it goes without saying!) and wrap them up.

Suggested menus

Spring

Game terrine with herb jelly *17*
Spaghetti with white crabmeat, olive oil, garlic, chilli and parsley *23*
Iced coffee cream cake with warm dark chocolate sauce *54*

Quails' eggs, avocado and crispy bacon salad with herb dressing *12*
Salmon fillets with watercress and shallot sauce *24*
Rhubarb and orange pistachio meringue pie with ginger pastry *44*

Lime-marinated fresh and smoked salmon in *crème fraîche*, dill
    and cucumber, with pink peppercorns *15*
Roast rack of lamb with pinhead oatmeal and a cracked black
    pepper crust, with minty Hollandaise sauce *33*
Warm fresh fruit salad in maple syrup with crisp ginger biscuits *41*

Potted crab with Melba toast *13*
Lamb shanks with shallots, raisins and red wine *35*
Seville orange curd and ginger ice cream with warm dark
    chocolate sauce *46*

Sautéed chicken livers with garlic, apples and balsamic vinegar *19*
Smoked haddock creamy stew with shallots, saffron and
    baby spinach *29*
Lime water ice with mango and ginger sauce *52*

Jerusalem artichoke soup with scallops *8*
Pork fillet with tomatoes, cream and Dijon mustard *32*
Almond lemon tart *49*

Marinated grilled aubergine slices with tomato and chilli sauce *21*
Hot-smoked salmon fishcakes with lime and shallot sauce *25*
Rhubarb and orange compote with crisp orange biscuits *43*

Roast red pepper, tomato and chilli soup *9*
Chicken and vegetable pie *30*
Crêpes suzette *47*

Spicy hummus with carrot sticks *20*
Baked marinated tuna steaks with Parmesan pasta *27*
Apple frangipane tart with lemon pastry *50*

Herb crêpes with smoked herring roe, cucumber and *crème fraîche* *16*
Venison fillet stir-fried with spring onions, red peppers, garlic,
    ginger and sesame oil *37*
Blueberry fool *40*

Blue cheese rarebit on fresh pears with fried walnuts *11*
Spicy red fish stew *28*
Espresso cream pots *53*

Broccoli and lemon soup *10*
Braised shin of beef with shallots, bacon, mushrooms and red wine *36*
Chocolate and toasted-nut squares *57*

Summer

Carrot and coriander soup with *crème fraîche* 64
Baked fillets of sea bass with lime chilli relish 78
Vanilla cream terrine with cinnamon cherries 110

Smoked venison with chicory leaves stuffed with cherries and
    horseradish *crème fraîche* 73
Fillets of cod baked with roast vine tomatoes, shallots and chilli 75
Baked strawberry and elderflower creams 107

Grated cucumber, chilli and lemon mousse 65
Chicken in roast ratatouille 83
Iced lemon meringue bombe 99

Asparagus and saffron risotto 74
Lime, sesame, ginger and garlic pork fillet stir-fry 85
Raspberry and toasted-almond meringue 102

Aubergine pâté with tomatoes and garlic 66
Pork fillet tonnato with tomato and caper salad 86
Lemon curd parfaits with raspberries 98

Grilled crab with asparagus 69
Cold spicy lemon and orange chicken 82
Strawberry and elderflower lemon curd tart 108

Cold spiced cucumber soup *63*
Pepper-crusted salmon fillets with tomato and basil salsa *76*
Carpaccio of pineapple with pineapple water ice *101*

Garlic-buttered langoustines *70*
Pork fillets with prune and sage stuffing, and prune, cream,
    shallot and sage sauce *88*
Blackcurrant leaf water ice with peach and raspberry compote *95*

Cold beetroot and orange soup with dill cream *62*
Baked aubergines with tomatoes, pesto, black olives
    and goat's cheese *93*
Gooseberry and elderflower compote with lemon marzipan cake *96*

Scallops stir-fried with spring onions, ginger and lime *71*
New potato salad with sugarsnaps, peas and asparagus
    with crispy bacon and thyme and lemon dressing *92*
Torta di Nonna *112*

Squid with garlic and parsley *72*
Warm chicken salad with chilli croûtes and a parsley dressing *80*
Strawberry and green peppercorn parfait *106*

Antipasti *67*
Pasta with red and yellow peppers, aubergines and basil *90*
Raspberry tart *104*

Autumn

Tagliolini with white Alba truffle *132*
Fillet of hake baked with roast aubergines and shallots, with aioli *138*
Orange-glazed apple and vanilla tart with orange and
    lemon pastry *165*

Spiced beetroot and carrot salad with garlic *122*
Chunky three-cheese tart with Parmesan pastry and
    pear and redcurrant sauce *158*
Bramble and blueberry compote with almond and lemon biscuits *166*

Twice-baked leek, goat's cheese and walnut soufflé *133*
Creamy fish and shellfish chowder *136*
Baked dark chocolate puddings *182*

Roast butternut squash and cumin soup *119*
Braised lamb with aubergines, red peppers, potatoes
    and chilli with garlic and coriander *151*
Baked bramble and fudge oatmeal and pecan crumble *167*

Tomato and red onion salad with green dressing *123*
Herb risotto with smoked haddock and grilled goat's cheese *140*
Hazelnut meringue with chocolate and apple purée *174*

Spicy cauliflower soup *120*
Venison fillet with wild mushroom sauce *156*
Baked dark and white chocolate cheesecake *178*

Leek and bacon timbales *135*
Baked pasta au gratin – mark two *152*
Pear, almond and vanilla clafoutis *171*

Baby spinach and sautéed mushroom salad with
    Parmesan croûtes *125*
Lamb and chorizo chilli *149*
Caramelized pineapple with caramelized pistachio nuts *170*

Spicy white bean salad *128*
Garlic croustade with leeks, Brie and pine nuts *160*
Honey-glazed baked apples stuffed with dates and raisins
    marinated in ginger wine and orange *164*

Wild mushroom consommé *118*
Marinated steaks with pepper cream sauce and roast root
    vegetables *154*
Dark chocolate and pecan tart *183*

Venison and prune terrine with Cumberland jelly *130*
Leek and bacon potato cakes, with tomato chilli sauce *141*
Pistachio ice cream *185*

Marinated olive and cherry tomato salad *127*
Braised lamb shanks with Puy lentils and pickled lemons *147*
Toasted coconut and vanilla sponge pudding with dark
    chocolate sauce *180*

Mussels with garlic, white wine and cream *129*
Potted wild duck with red onion, orange and mixed-leaf salad *143*
Hazelnut roulade with vanilla *crème pâtissière* and brambles *176*

Baked spinach purée with Parmesan *134*
Pork fillets with apples, onions, cider and cream, with red cabbage
    braised with rowanberries *145*
Baked damson and lemon pudding *168*

Tomato, pear and horseradish soup *121*
Pot-roast rabbit with root vegetables *153*
Spiced panna cotta with marinated raisins in apple purée *172*

Winter

Sweet potato, lime and ginger soup *190*
Tartiflette *217*
Pink grapefruit and Campari jellied terrine, with pink grapefruit
    and orange compote, with caramelized peel *233*

Oxtail and root vegetable stew *228*
Vanilla panna cotta with Seville orange compote *243*

Marinated marmalade-glazed pork sausages with onion
    marmalade, and with butter-steamed Savoy cabbage *220*
Cinnamon ice cream with baked gingerbread and
    black pepper pudding *252*

Leek and mushroom salad with toasted pine nuts *200*
Roast loin of pork with roast apples, shallots and juniper *222*
Panettone and apricot Marsala trifle *241*

Beetroot remoulade *201*
Ham, boiled and roast, with shallot, red wine and orange sauce *218*
Dark chocolate crème brûlée, with crystallized pink
    grapefruit peel *246*

Marinated figs and rocket salad, with grilled goat's cheese *199*
Eggs Benedict *206*
Baked blueberry, lemon and almond pudding *235*

Leek and chicken soup with blanched lemon peel *191*
Hot-smoked salmon kedgeree with quails' eggs *209*
Iced Christmas bombe *249*

Orange, mint and olive salad with cumin dressing *197*
Venison pudding with lemon suet crust *230*
Egg nog mousse *251*

Potted cheese with watercress and red onion salad
   with walnut dressing *195*
Seville orange and soy sauce marinated pheasant breasts *215*
Baked orange and lemon pudding with spiced cranberries *238*

Spicy courgette fritters with tomato and chive mayonnaise *203*
Braised pork with mushrooms, garlic and red wine *224*
Baked lemon cream rice pudding *240*

Watercress, pink grapefruit and red onion salad with vinaigrette *198*
Roast duck with ginger, port and green peppercorn sauce *211*
Dark chocolate and cinnamon ice *248*

Baked butternut squash, onion and parsnip au gratin *205*
Scallops with Jerusalem artichokes and leeks *208*
Sliced clementines in caramel with caramel cream *232*

Baked Brie with an almond and Demerara sugar crust served
   with grape salsa *193*
Winter navarin of lamb *226*
Baked spiced apricot fudge pudding *236*

Smoked salmon with Avruga *crème fraîche* *196*
Roast goose with prune, apple and lemon stuffing *213*
Vanilla meringue with dark chocolate cream and marrons glacés *244*

Index